THE
DYNAMICS
OF HOPE

BOOKS BY IRA PROGOFF

At a Journal Workshop:
The Basic Text and Guide for Using the *Intensive Journal* Process

The Practice of Process Meditation:
The *Intensive Journal* Way to Spiritual Experience

Life-Study:
Experiencing Creative Lives by the *Intensive Journal* Method

The Well and the Cathedral

The White Robed Monk

The Star/Cross

The Death and Rebirth of Psychology

Depth Psychology and Modern Man

The Symbolic and the Real

Jung's Psychology and Its Social Meaning

Jung, Synchronicity and Human Destiny

The Image of an Oracle

THE DYNAMICS OF HOPE

Perspectives of Process
in
Anxiety and Creativity, Imagery and Dreams

Ira Progoff

DIALOGUE HOUSE LIBRARY/NEW YORK

Published by
Dialogue House Library
80 East Eleventh Street
New York, New York 10003

Copyright © 1985 by Ira Progoff

Intensive Journal® is a registered trademark of
Dr. Ira Progoff and is used under license by
Dialogue House Associates, Inc.

Library of Congress Catalog Card Number: 85-16236

ISBN 0-87941-013-2

Printed in the United States of America

SECOND PRINTING 1987

Dedicated to the memory of
OLGA FROEBE-KAPTEYN
Founder and nurturer of
the Eranos Tagung, Ascona, Switzerland

Contents

APPENDIX

INTRODUCTION

Between
Hope and Anxiety

In the back and forth movement between hope and anxiety, the personal relationships and the work involvements that comprise a life are formed. One by one, as they take shape, they cumulatively build the artwork that is each individual's life, for the most important artwork of all is the life of a person. On the outer level, these works and relationships are the tangible contents of a life. On the interior level their continuity and connections carry the theme, the goals and activities by which the meaning of each life evolves. This is the opus of the life, the inner meaning of the life, what the person privately feels the life is *for*.

The nature of the opus of a life, carrying its inner meaning, is that it unfolds as the life proceeds. It is not apparent at the beginning, but it fills in its content as the events of the life take place. Sometimes, although a great deal seems to be happening on the surface of the life, very little is being added to the opus. Sometimes, although very little seems to be taking place on the outside, the opus of the life is being built significantly within. This is because it often is indeed true that still water runs deep. Before an individual has indicated the commitments of the life, when the life is just starting, the opus that carries the meaning of the life is not present yet as an actuality that can be seen. It is there only as a seed-potential. The person may then have intimations of what may possibly unfold in the future; but it can be no more than an intimation at the beginning. It is only after several cycles of experience have been lived through that the opus of a life begins to be visible in actuality.

In their movement the several cycles may take a person back and forth again and again between the opposites of hope and anxiety. Often this is felt to be a repetitive process in the life because the same contents that appeared in an early phase of the life appear again in a later cycle. When the contents reappear, however, we have to look closely to see what their present phase of development may be; and what the present context of our life is now, for it is the current context in which they are reappearing. Outwardly they may appear to be the same as they used to be but they may now be much further along in their own process of development, and they may now be ready to play a much different role in our lives than in the past. We need to pay attention in order that we can hear and respond to their new message for our life. When we do, we perceive that the contents of our lives move through their own specific cycles within the larger cycles of our lives as a whole. It is as though there are lives within our individual life. Continuities are unfolding within us even while the cycles of experience within which they were germinating come to a close. While particular aspects of our lives come to an end, other aspects continue their development and move toward further levels of fulfillment. We may be experiencing frustration in one area of our life while a new strength is germinating and growing in another area. There is a diversity of rhythms in the movements taking place within us as individuals, for the contents of a life in modern civilization are multiple.

This is a very hopeful and helpful fact, for there are several sources of energy, both inner sources and social sources, active in the life of a person at any one time. When there is an ending, experienced as a failure, in one area of energy, there may be growth and development reinforcing the person in another area. The sources of energy are multiple, but it is a single individual who is being formed by the continuity of inner and outer events moving in the life of the person at a level beyond consciousness. A single person is being formed with a destiny unique to that individual. The person being formed is the embodiment of the meaning of that life. That is the opus of the life: what the person perceives qualitatively as the meaning and value of his or her life. These experiences lead to the development of individuals, but cumulatively they form the atmosphere and the meaning of a civilization.

In this perspective there are two kinds of understanding that are needed. At a fundamental level a conceptual understanding is necessary in order to identify the contents and the movements taking place within a human life. And derived from this, a practical understanding is needed in order to provide the methods by which a sense of wholeness and qualitative values in a human existence can be built and become an actuality. The conceptual phase of this understanding has come to me in the format of depth psychology as I have worked with it on theoretical levels. The practical understanding has come to me through the use of the *Intensive Journal* process and especially of the method of Journal Feedback in my own and other person's lives.

The papers brought together in this volume are primarily devoted to building the conceptual framework that underlies the practical work of the *Intensive Journal* process. The two large papers given here are the main parts of the presentations made at the Eranos Tagung (conference) in Ascona, Switzerland in August 1963 and in 1965. Each was originally given as a talk to the conference and was later printed in enlarged form in the Eranos Jahrbuch for that year. The continuity of thought linking the two papers provided the fundamental concepts with which the *Intensive Journal* process could be made and with which eventually the various *Intensive Journal* methods of individual life-development could be devised. The concepts contained in these papers therefore inherently led to implementation. Their nature is conceptual, but mainly in order to provide a valid base on which a practical program of personal development could be built. By the word "practical" I mean individual development carried out in a way that feeds into the society as a whole. That has been the focus of my attention since the *Intensive Journal* process was first developed, and it has led to the social programs for the individual use of the *Intensive Journal* process that are now in existence. As the applications of method are increasing, it becomes all-the-more important that we remind ourselves of the concepts that underlie the methods. The papers that are presented here are a step in this direction. There are more to follow, for both the purposes of further study of what has been done and for consideration of what may be developed in the future.

In the light of what has transpired during the past two decades, it seems clear to me now that there are three aspects of theory on which the concepts and methodology of the *Intensive Journal* process have been based. These are:

1) *Dialectics*, the tendency of opposites to form and build the energies of movement within a human existence.

2) *Depth*, the dimension of human experience that expresses itself by means of symbols, as we see both in sleep dreams and in waking dreams. A significant aspect of this is imaging, with the equivalent phrase for depth, "the twilight range," often used in *Intensive Journal* work.

3) *Holistic Integration*, the tendency of the life process both in the world of nature and in human society, to form new and ever more refined units, or integrations, of life. Since the nature of these new integrations is that they are "emergents" of life that were never in existence before and could not be consciously planned, the word, *creative*, applies here. Drawing on Dialectics and Depth, Holistic Integration is a key to creativity.

The first two of these, Dialectics and Depth, are discussed in the 1963 and 1965 Eranos papers in this volume, and there is particular reference to the aspects of Twilight Imaging in the papers of Part III. The third principle, that of Holistic Integration, is not discussed explicitly on the level of concept in the papers of this volume. It is present implicitly, however, but primarily in the sense that it is inherent in the process by which dialectical and depth factors combine to form new units and new directions in a life.

With regard to Holistic Integration, the fact is that it was only after the early period of *Intensive Journal* usage indicated that the theories of Jan Christian Smuts were spontaneously being incorporated into the *Intensive Journal* process (particularly by the clustering of brief entries in Journal Feedback) that the *holistic* conception was given a fundamental place in the *Intensive Journal* process. It had been there implicitly all the while, but now there could be explicit procedures for using it. Specifically, as dialectical factors are seen in the context of their process of moving from one phase of their life in the direction of their opposite, *Intensive Journal* methods used at a twilight level make it possible to draw them through their cycles and evoke the messages they are carrying for the future. The concepts that are spoken of in the papers of this volume provide the terms in which we will individually see aspects of our lives from an intellectual point of view. When we feed them into the *Intensive Journal* process, however, they combine with other factors to form new integrations by means of Journal Feedback, thus providing the terms for the next step in our lives. Although their contents may be stated in the terms of concepts that we find here, the new integrations come about nonanalytically and their messages for us are written in our own handwriting as we proceed in the *Intensive Journal* process.

The movement from hope to anxiety and back again is a ubiquitous cycle in human experience. It is essential in the process of creativity, but parts of it are often labelled as neurosis. It is a movement from a constructive aspect of human life into its opposite. Linking the two and building the tension between them is the dialectical factor, the tendency for opposites to form in the midst of life. In the case of hope and anxiety the basis on which the opposites form is primarily a difference in timing that arises from the phases of hoping. When a person experiences hope, there comes with it an image of something that is to be given tangible form in the outer world. It is for the future, and it is envisioned whole. The problem arises from the fact that the imagery and the experience of hope are interior. Interior time, being experienced at a depth level, tends to be rapid; but the movement of time externally is chronological time, and it moves as slowly as the clock and calendar move. When an image that has been perceived at an interior level is being converted into an external form, the differences in timing are experienced. That is when the Dialectic of Inner and Outer gives rise to the tension of time and to the conflicts and other difficulties that arise within a person.

There is a point in the Dialectic of Hope and Anxiety where a vacuum forms. Something has been spontaneously hoped for and has been expressed in images that give it specific form; but the feeling of anxiety that arises within the person says that it will never happen in actuality. It is a fear that forms in the midst of the act of hoping, and it creates a vacuum within the person. This vacuum is a painful place in which to find oneself. It is an empty space that belongs neither to the past nor to the future. Certainly we have a right to feel anxiety when we find ourselves in such a position. At such a time, we are neither here nor there.

We can, however, experience hope in a way that leads beyond anxiety. That is what the *Intensive Journal* method seeks to make possible in practice. It provides as our instrument the *Intensive Journal* workbook so that we can work privately with those of its exercises that fit our life situation. As we proceed we realize that there are several lines of continuity in our lives and that these together constitute our individual present moment. We find that our present is both single and multiple. From it, by means of the Journal exercises we reach out both into the past and into the future. We do this at a depth level that is beyond consciousness, and it is here that we find the varied implications as well as the potentials of what the Now Moment holds for us. We are able to experience the Dialectic of Hope and Anxiety actively in our lives with a perspective that includes anxiety but that keeps us beyond the reach of its painful sting. It is in this sense that the *Intensive Journal* method moves by means of the dialectics of human existence to a place that is beyond the opposites while it maintains our contact with the actualities of our lives.

In certain aspects of the movement into opposites, the dialectical factor in life has very negative effects. It can be exceedingly discouraging to individuals who are caught by the negative aspects of its dynamic. It can be especially discouraging, and disconcerting too, when a person is caught in the lower phase of a movement of opposites and loses perspective. One does not know what to do then. It becomes very easy to believe that all the contents of one's life are lost, or are about to be lost.

When, for example, the dialectic of life is turning the enthusiasms of hope into the fears of anxiety and is giving the frightening feeling that what one had been hoping for will "never" come to pass, the person is placed in the position of viewing life from the very bottom of a cycle. The movement into opposites, the movement from a positive to a negative as from hope to anxiety, necessarily goes in cycles. The downward part that moves from the affirmative to the negative is one half of the cycle but the nature of a cycle is that it contains two parts. After moving downward and reaching bottom, it remains in this "valley" phase for an indeterminate period—for as long as its contents require—and then, without being prodded from the outside but moving in its own timing, it reverses direction. It moves back upward again, going once again into its opposite. This time it is moving into the opposite of anxiety.

In observing the experience of human beings in modern civilization and in considering the lives of persons who lived in earlier times of history, we see that this cycle of movement into opposites, either in its downward or its upward phase, constitutes a very large part of human life. When a person is at the bottom of the cycle, in its valley phase, the world is necessarily viewed from the bottom up. It gives a worm's eye view of human life. But that is not all that there is to the cycle. That is only the first half; and there is a second half as well. Looking closely at the life experiences of many persons, we see that the outcome of the second movement of opposites—the movement upward from the valley—tends to place a person in a different psychological position than at the starting point. The changes take place during the two phases of the cycle of opposites, the downward and upward movements, and during the time in-between. At the beginning there is the movement downward from hope to anxiety; then there is the time in-between, the time of waiting. This is the time in the valley when there seems to be no movement at all taking place, at least none on the outer level that can be seen; and thirdly there is the movement upward from the valley of anxiety to another opposite.

The culmination of this phase of the cycle can also be seen as a positive, as was the beginning of the process from which the movement into opposites began. But the culmination is different from the beginning. Something seems to happen in the course of the cyclical movement of opposites. The movement that goes first downward and then upward again is not unaffected by the fact of its twofold movement. Having gone from hope to anxiety, it is not the same when it leaves the phase of anxiety and reaches a positive pole once again. It has then completed two movements of opposites, both the downward and the upward phases of a cycle of experience, and it is now in a different place than it was when it began. It may be that this change is what William Blake had in mind when he spoke of the difference between "innocence" and "experience".

Something happens that changes things and leads to a new outcome when a person continues and moves through the downward and upward phases and covers a full cycle of experience. The first is the movement downward into a valley of anxiety where feelings of unsureness are experienced. It seems to be during this low time of anxiety that the changes and further developments in a person take place. But, of course, if the anxiety is diagnosed and treated and eliminated, the further developments in the person will not take place since it is the dynamic factor in the process that has been treated and eliminated. Further, since the changes in the person involve enlargements in awareness and in the person's capacities for absorbing and responding to the events of life, it is necessary to move through both phases of the cycle in order to experience the full process. If the impact of the cycle is softened by a mollifying treatment, the pain of the anxiety will be avoided and so also will the experience of personal deepening and strengthening with its consequent growth in consciousness.

It is important that we bear both phases of the cycle of experience in mind when we are passing through the vicissitudes of our lives. If we eliminate one phase of our experience because it is unpleasant, we may also be eliminating a phase of experience that we desire. It is essential that we maintain our awareness of the process as a whole so that we do not cut it short. One of the functions of the *Intensive Journal* workbook with its exercises is to give us an instrument with which we can maintain our perspective as we move through the valley of anxiety—whatever its particular content in our life—until we reach the upward phase of the cycle where the oppostites will renew themselves.

In this context it is helpful for us to have, as a symbol of the movement of process in our lives, a perspective of the cycles that occur in the world of nature. In nature we see the movement of opposites all around us. Daylight gradually fades and becomes its opposite. Once there, the light remains in darkness for an indeterminate time—for as long as is necessary depending on the season—and then there is a movement upward toward the opposite to become light again. Thus a unit is formed in which a full cycle is completed in the world of nature, a time of light, a time of darkness, and a time of light again, one full day. The equivalent of this is true of the passage of the seasons and of those plants and animals in the state of nature whose lives are governed by the seasons. First a movement takes place in one direction toward the opposite of the starting point; then a pause, a resting, a waiting. And then a movement back up and toward an opposite again, the beginning of a new day. That is the basic cycle of opposites in the state of nature.

The continuity of the process of life includes these cycles moving in succession, one after another, but at a certain point in the evolution of nature we notice a significant change. At the point where human beings move out of the state of nature and evolve from the simpler societies into the condition of civilization, they become conscious of their lives as individuals. In various forms that is when self-consciousness begins. It enters history as a derivative of the condition in society in which human beings live as individuals in a state of civilization. Self-consciousness is a definite advancement in the evolution of human life. But we know also that being conscious of one's individuality places a limitation on the flow of creativity that led to individuality in the first place. Self-consciousness also leads to an awareness that the main developments in our consciousness are taking place *behind our minds* at nonconscious levels. We recognize that our capacities of consciousness are derived from unconscious processes, and further, that these processes move dialectically within us, in each case moving toward their opposite. The self-consciousness that has developed in us as human beings who live in a state of civilization leads us to realize that our present condition is a phase of a larger movement of opposites that is taking place in the depth of us. As individuals seeking to develop the capacities of our consciousness we require the means of placing ourselves in a harmonious relationship both with these unconscious sources themselves and with the process of cyclic movement into their opposite. They are inevitably drawn into the cyclic movement into opposites, but it is not sufficient to say that we know this. As the movement is taking place in the specifics of its process, it generates messages that are of value for our life as a whole. It is essential that we receive these messages, consider them and learn from them. Usually it is a case of the part speaking to the whole, often with great intuitive, even precognitive, relevance. But the messages are given in the depth of us, in the twilight range of our experience, often presented in symbolic forms. How shall we find out what they are telling us? We can do this by following their leads into the various sections and sub-sections of our *Intensive Journal* workbook. There, as they come together in clusters with other Journal Feedback leads, they nonanalytically form new integrations of perception that open new vistas of experience and new directions for our lives.

The messages are formed in the depth of us while we are in the midst of the cycles of experience that carry us through the valley of the opposites. While in that valley, we are in the depths of our being. It is a twilight place where significant symbols both of our personal and our more-than-personal life can be shown to us; and these awarenesses, drawn from our time in the depth, can become a resource for our activities on the outer level of life. A great deal of creativity is involved in this, both for the specific works of a life and for the atmosphere that changes attitudes and opens windows of new awareness for the person. That atmosphere can be established, and sometimes establishes itself, at the depth level of human existence. In various formats and situations, the concepts and practices that make it possible to establish this atmosphere is what the papers in this volume are about.

For the most part the discussions are reprinted here as they were originally published. Our primary purpose in drawing them together in this format is to elucidate our understanding of the principles that underlie *Intensive Journal* work. With this in mind, comments and explanations have been inserted in the text from time to time, especially in footnotes. Some larger additions have also been made. One of these is the extended discussion of the dream that recapitulated the life of Leo Tolstoy. Another is the description of the incident in which a transforming use was made of Biblical symbolism. A third is the discussion of Utopian Persons at the close of Part I. Other extended comments are placed in the Appendix.

PART ONE

The Dynamics of Hope and the Utopian Person (Eranos, 1963)

1

Hope
and Utopia

Utopia is to society what hope is to the individual. It is an image of the future as one would wish the future to be. From the psychological point of view, the personal images in which hope is embodied present themselves in the form of dreams, sleep dreams and waking dreams. In a corresponding sense, utopia is a dream. Utopia and hope are both visions of reality that come ahead of time. The implications of this are important to understand, for fundamental aspects of the human psyche are expressed in it. Let us begin therefore by inquiring what is implied when we speak of an image of reality. And let us then ask what it means to come ahead of time.

What is an image of reality? We should state it here as briefly and as simply as we can. An image of reality is a symbolic expression of something that is true in essence but is not necessarily true in fact. It is not something that is established in outer experience, but it is true in principle. It is something that is real primarily in its essence.

This is an ideal, but it is also practical because it has become part of the human being's experience not merely as an abstraction but with the implication that it will eventually be translated into the realities of life. In other words, the vision of reality that is given carries with it two different aspects of reality: the first is what is real in principle, as an abstraction and as a goal; and the other is the possibility of a reality that can be lived concretely in the world.

At this point, however, where it is about to become a practical fact, the image of reality must be understood as a *potentiality*. This means that it is something that is capable of becoming concrete, but that its time is not yet. And so the image comes ahead of time. It comes before it can be made real in the world; but it comes ahead of time precisely in order that it can become real eventually, in order that the guiding principle of growth can be present and can be active in working toward fulfilling itself.

In this sequence, the most appropriate metaphor is to speak of the acorn as though it could dream. In its dreams there would be presented to it visually the oak tree that is folded up inside the acorn as the form and limit of its potentiality. Or again, it is as if a tulip bulb could dream. Its dream would be of the tulip flower, and of the states of growth and of impediment by which that flower would come into being.

If the acorn or the tulip could dream, if the seed of any being could dream, its dream would be an image of what is present within it, latently, waiting more or less patiently or impatiently for the time when it can make good the promise of its existence. The nature of the dream is that its time is not yet but that its time will be. This does not mean that the dream is an unconscious wish, nor that it is an expression of will power moving toward consciousness. It is rather a reflection of the future while the future is still contained in the womb of potentiality. It is a symbolic fore-visioning brought forth from the depths by which one receives intimations ahead of time of what is stirring in the dark center of the seed. When the time for fulfillment comes, the dream will be much less symbolic; it will be much more specific in making actual what is already present as the promise in the seed. As

Meister Eckhart says, "Pear seeds grow into pear trees; nut seeds into nut trees; and God seeds into God."*

When a human being dreams the equivalent of the acorn's dream of the oak tree, that is its image of reality. That is the image of the ultimate potentiality that is possible for it as a particular form of life.

A primary psychological principle is contained in this. The metaphor that we have used, and the comparison quoted from Eckhart, only serve to emphasize the fact that psychological principles, which eventually become spiritual principles when their implications are fulfilled, are reflections of the patterns of life as these patterns are expressed in the world of nature.

In the human individual the dream image, or a waking image of reality in any other form, comes first. It comes before the event; but it opens the way for the events to unfold in the direction of fulfilling the potentiality that is in the seed. This is true of individuals, as it is true of plants and trees; and it is true also of societies. For societies also move forward in terms of dreams or visions of reality that carry the image of potentiality by which the meaning of a given society can be fulfilled. It may even be that human society as a whole has such an image implicit in the seed of its being, implicit in the social nature of mankind. It may be that this image has been dreamed imperfectly in the past, has been dreamed many times in the past, and that it needs to be dreamed again and again until it can become a reality of history. These dreams are the stuff of which utopia is made, first in the individuals who have the visions and then in the society as a whole.

In all of this, in the process of growth in nature, in the human individual, and in society, there is an inherent tension. It is a tension of time which expresses an essential as-

---

*Meister Eckhart: A Modern Translation by R. B. Blakney, Harper Torchbooks, New York, p. 75.

pect of the process of growth in all living things, and it is
certainly at the very core of the human psyche. The tension of
time is a tension, on the one hand, between the future which
is not yet but which is already present as an image of potentiality although still unformed and therefore without limitation; and, on the other hand, the bounded and limited
situation of the present. The future is bursting to come
through, but it cannot because its time is not yet. Nonetheless, it must continue to press until it bursts the bounds of
the present moment. This tension of time is the essence of all
creativity by which what is new presses until it eventually
breaks itself out of the shell that contains it. To work out
one's personal relation to this tension of time seems to be a
primary psychological task for the developed human being.
One has to learn how to be an instrument for the future
while living contained within the limitations and frustrations
of an environment that still bears the stamp of the past. The
present moment is moving toward the future, but it does so
while it is still encompassed by the quality and atmosphere
of the past. Thus both the opposites of life with respect to
time are within it. This is the tension of time that is inherent
in every moment in which something creative and new is
being formed and is being prepared for life.

There is an image of potentiality that inheres in any given
society, and that image comes forth in the form of a vision or
in the symbolism of a dream. But a society cannot have a
dream; only an individual can have a dream, or see a vision,
or proclaim a prophecy. For this reason the visions that express the inner meaning and possibility, that forecast the
next step for a society, come by means of individuals. There
is great significance, therefore, in the relation between the
society as a whole and the individual persons who have the
visions which articulate the meaning and destiny of each
particular culture.

These visionaries, or prophets, or artists, as they may be,

have their visions for themselves and out of their own inner need, but they also have them on behalf of their society and their fellow human beings. In fact, this is one of the characteristics of the type of persons whom we may call *Utopian Persons*. These are individuals who do not experience their personal good as separate from that of the community. Their inner perception is, rather, that the fulfillment of high goals of life for their fellow human beings is identical with the well being and the purpose of their own existence. In fact, it is not uncommon for such persons to be blocked and disturbed in their individual lives until they reach a point where they can feel that their lives are connected to a social meaning. It will be very instructive for us to see what is involved psychologically in the experience of such persons, and especially in the dynamics of the process by which their visions of reality come to them. The visions of such persons constitute the great social hopes of the community, but they are social hopes that are individually experienced. We want to see, therefore, what leads up to the image of utopia as a psychological experience, what its contents are from the cultural point of view, and what its implications may be for the situation of man in modern civilization.

2

Participating
in Biblical Symbolism

Implicit in the image of utopia is a vision of what is highest and best in man. It, therefore, includes aspects that are both personal and more than personal. The primary contents of utopian imagery are *transpersonal*, but this term must be understood in a large and flexible and nondogmatic sense. It has various levels, none of which can be strictly defined since the meaning of each depends not only on its intellectual context but on the subjective tone with which it is experienced. The term *transpersonal* may refer to what is more than personal simply in a social sense; further, it may touch what is more than personal in the larger sense of what is generically, or universally human; or, beyond that, it may be referring to that aspect of human existence that is beyond man, that is ontologically transpersonal. In point of fact, none of these is mutually exclusive of the others. All are actually implicit in the term depending on the quality of experience that is present in the individual.

To understand what is involved in this, we must maintain a large cultural perspective. We must bear in mind that every major civilization contains at least one large and encompassing tradition of thought that bears the characteristic stamp of that civilization. In this there is contained for each culture a great treasury of images, a reservoir of symbols and meanings that have been slowly, imperceptively accumulated since the primordial origins of the civilization, gradually setting the tone of its philosophies and mythologies of life. In each culture and at all the moving points of its history, individuals draw upon this reservoir. Spontaneously, and without realizing that they are doing so, they draw specific symbols from the cultural past and adapt them as their own in shaping their beliefs about life and in giving direction to their personal existence. Most individuals gain access to this collective source of symbols by the obvious and established channels, namely, through the traditional religion, the literature, and the ritual observances of the culture. Others, however, make contact with their historical sources in less obvious and less visible ways: they use the channels of the inner life, sometimes in the midst of great conflict and in intense psychological pain. For these individuals, the major and effective symbols become accessible through their dreams, their visions, and other experiences which on one level are subjective to them but which also involve a stirring and awakening of the more-than-individual depths of personality that pertains to the community as a whole.

These inner events tend to be cast in terms of imagery, either visual or non-visual in style. They are symbolic; but very often, when individuals are totally encompassed by the symbolic patterns of their culture, the symbols in which they believe seem to them to be so self-evidently true that they regard them as the literal and absolute realities of life. In a variety of symbolic forms, from ancient days to our modern culture, individuals have had, by means of dreams and other seemingly subjective symbolic perceptions, intense inner contacts with the ultimate meanings of life; and these have brought a great power into both their personal lives and into the life of their culture.

Inward encounters of this kind are a primary source of

those individual acts of inspiration in religion, in poetry, and in science, that cumulatively build in the course of history the cultural heritage of a people. These acts of inspiration are personal in the sense that they happen only to individuals; but they are also non-personal—or transpersonal—in the sense that their contents, their subject matter, and the quality of their insights, relate to more than the individual; they involve the essentials and the universals of human existence. They are transpersonal also in the sense that they cannot be brought about deliberately by an act of conscious will. They are beyond individual control, and when they are experienced the imagery by which they are carried tends to be more than personal in tone. They touch the ultimates and the universals of life, as the perception of "infinity in a grain of sand," or the opening of vision beyond the boundaries of hourly time. Awareness of existence in the light of eternity carries with it overtones of spirit. It may indeed be that this breaking open of the walls of time in the act of symbolic perception is a main aspect of what is being indicated when such experiences are referred to as *spiritual* experiences.

Some experiences of this kind are abstract perceptions of existence without specific symbolic content; but others are very definite in their symbolism. This is particularly true of those religious experiences in which the individual perceives the reality of his own life in terms of the symbols of a cultural tradition. The tendency for such persons is that they enrich their feeling of the reality of the present by reliving an event of the mythological or historical past in such a way that it comes alive again in their own existence.

There are many examples of this in primitive cultures. Before embarking on a hunt, for example, it has been common for a ritual to be performed in which the purpose is to invoke the god who governs the hunt. Psychologically the goal of the ritual is to establish an atmosphere in which the men of the tribe feel that they are following in the footsteps of their great divine precursor, the prototype of all hunters. They are brought into a frame of mind in which each feels that he is reenacting and therefore emulating the behavior of the god, hunting as *he* had hunted in the dim primordial days when the gods were living out their lives on earth. Thus, as the ritual takes effect, they feel that the god is living in and through them when they go out on the hunt, and they feel sustained and protected from danger by his power.

More sophisticated instances of this occur in western civilization whenever, for whatever reason, an individual meditates deeply enough upon a Biblical character to experience that life as a prototype of his own modern existence. Then, as in the case of the primitive ritual, a transformation of consciousness is brought about. It is a transformation in the sense that it provides a new and larger perspective in which to see the situation of the life. The actuality of the events remain the same, but the circumstances are reset in a context of universality and timelessness. Then the situation of the life, which had been experienced as encompassing and enclosing the person, is loosened, giving the person psychological breathing space and opening new possibilities. In the phrase of Benedict Spinoza the situation can then be seen *sub specie eternitatis*, in the light of eternity, perceived in symbolic forms that are readily translatable into the terms of one's own life.

In the course of my years of practicing psychotherapy I have been party on many occasions to the experience of entering into Biblical symbolism as a means of finding a larger dimension for a modern life. I recall the experience of a young man who was consulting me because of sexual habit patterns that he felt were destroying the potentials of his life. One night, while out carousing, he was set upon by three hoodlums who beat and robbed him. Left half unconscious in an alleyway, he finally arose and wandered the streets in a daze, eventually finding his way to a hospital where he received the necessary treatment and his broken arm was set in a cast.

A few days later when he came to talk with me he was not only still in a state of shock, but also severely depressed. He could see in this irrational, totally unprovoked attack nothing but another instance of the misfortunes that seemed ever to be his lot in life. To him it was only an additional indication of the fact of which he had already been convinced, namely, that his was to be a tragic destiny, that his life would continue to be filled with failure and pain in the future as it had been in the past. Thus the feelings of depression deepened in him as the aftermath of the assault.

I asked him what situations he could think of in history or in literature that paralleled the event that had befallen him. He mentioned some thoughts and associations that strayed into his mind. Then the name of Jacob was mentioned. Although he was not a religious person in a church-going sense, he was familiar with the Biblical story and we talked about it. After a time, as the parallels became increasingly relevant to him, I drew out a copy of the Bible and together we read the passage in the Book of Genesis where Jacob's struggle with the angel is described.

He was deeply moved by the story; it clearly "spoke to his condition." I then read the story aloud to him again while he closed his eyes. I suggested that he relax as much as he could under the circumstances and that he permit himself to visualize the events taking place and to see them upon an inner screen, looking at them with his mind's eye. (This is an adaptation of the technique I have called *twilight imaging*.)* Presently the inward atmosphere intensified sufficiently that he could feel himself to be there, engaged in Jacob's struggle,

---

*For a description and examples of "twilight imaging" see Progoff, *The Symbolic and the Real*, McGraw Hill, N.Y., pages 109ff. See also, Progoff, *At a Journal Workshop*, p. 77ff.

feeling the fright of it, the danger, the confusion, the pain and the determination not to surrender—all that was involved in the struggle. When this phase of the "twilight imaging" was completed and our session was brought to a close, the young man went home with the "assignment" that he enter into the event of Jacob's struggle again in his own privacy. He was to enter into it until the symbolism of the event became "real" to him, so real that he could actually be there and experience his own modern existence in its terms.

He was able to do that, and without very great difficulty. When he went home he described in his "psychological workbook"* the imaging experience he had had in my office, and as he wrote about it he entered into Jacob's struggle with the angel once again, continuing and extending it as he wrote. Increasingly Jacob's struggle became his own and the three hoodlums who had accosted him became representatives of God as it had been in the Bible.

The Biblical event became his own modern encounter. The fear and the struggle through which he had lived were present once again, but now they were experienced within the framework of another dimension of reality. He was reliving it within the symbolism of the Jacobean encounter, and thus his own presence now had a different quality. He himself, the protagonist, was changed. The bloody event in the alleyway had spontaneously transfigured itself so that it became the embodiment of his encounter with the transpersonal powers affecting the meaning of his life. It had embodied itself as an actual event taking place in the outer world; and it was also an inward event taking place in the

---

*The Psychological Workbook referred to here as used in this instance is the unstructured form of the diary that preceded the *Intensive Journal* process. In later developments this became the *Intensive Journal* workbook with sectional divisions used as the basis of the Journal Feedback method as described in *At a Journal Workshop* and subsequent books. It has become the basis for the National *Intensive Journal* Program.

depths of his being. Both aspects were true at the same time, and they were united by the symbolic quality of the two events, the Biblical one and the modern one, so that they could move into each other and illuminate each other. They were united by their symbolism, and it was this symbolic quality that transfigured both of them and raised them to a level that enabled the young man to experience the reality of their symbolism. They were real to him with implications reaching through their symbolism to the actualities of his life.

As he was present in the image—and it was now an old/new image, for it was both modern and ancient at the same time—its symbolism became a reality and carried him on. There was a blessing to be given. That had been the outcome and the meaning of Jacob's struggle, for Jacob had struggled until the blessing had come. Now he too would continue to struggle until a blessing would be given him. He remained within the experience of the image until a blessing did come to him.

It came in the form of an inner assurance that the hoodlums' outer attack was the token of a transformation to take place within him, as had been the case for Jacob. He felt a change in the quality of his consciousness being brought about by his twofold experience of the symbol, through its outer form and inwardly, and by the stretching effect of reaching across time to a timeless reality. He felt also, and it seemed at the time to be almost incidental in his mind, that in the course of the blessing of his inner transformation he would be freed from the compulsive habit that was making his life so difficult. Shortly afterwards, when he was going to the hospital to have the doctor take the cast off, a curious punning quality of his mind told him that this would also be the time when he would "cast off" his habit. And so it was.

3
The Principle
of Symbolic Unfoldment

The incident described above despite its limited frame of reference of a single troubled life, demonstrates the presence of a factor that is of great importance in depth psychology. It is the principle of *symbolic unfoldment* which affects the mode in which the pattern of growth takes place within symbols in relation to the levels of depth in the life experience of individuals.

Experience in working with the imaginative faculties has directed attention to a principle of movement within symbols that is a major factor in their functioning. The awareness of this begins with the observation that there are different degrees or levels at which symbols are effective. At a relatively superficial level, for example, a symbol will be meaningful in terms of the memories of personal life and of associations connected with it. At successively deeper levels, however, its meanings reach out beyond individuality and express intimations of more fundamental aspects of human existence.

We can see the extent of these gradations even in so ubiquitous a symbol as the tree. On the personal level, a particular tree may be symbolic to an individual of a past experience, painful or pleasurable; or it may call up a childhood memory with strong emotion. Again, in more subtle terms, a tree in a dream may be symbolic of the relationship to one's parents or to other figures of authority in the community. Going somewhat more deeply, the tree may be the symbolic carrier of an appreciation of nature and, even more, of a feeling of connection to life, as in the moving though sentimental poem of Joyce Kilmer. "Poems are made by fools like me; but only God can make a tree."

Going further but remaining on the social level of symbols, is the traditional association of the tree with the fall of man, sexual temptation, and the knowledge of good and evil. Within this same social context, however, the tree symbol goes deeper and reaches beyond itself as it speaks of the Tree of Life that is guarded and remains beyond mankind but as a presence symbolic of life. An example of the active social experience of the symbol of the tree is found in the history of the Zionist movement preparatory to the founding of the state of Israel when the planting of trees became a sacramental act reclaiming the land in fulfillment of a religious prophecy.

On a still deeper level, beyond special social contexts is the symbol of the tree as an expression of the totality and inner essence of the life process itself. Sometimes this is perceived in personal terms. For example, in a dream that I reported in *The Symbolic and the Real*, a misshapen tree appeared as a representation of the distorted development of the individual's past life. Upon it there hung a golden key pointing to the treasure which his future contained buried at the foot of this misshapen tree of his life.

Deeper than the personal and reaching toward the ultimates of existence is the appearance of the tree as an encompassing symbol for studying the mysteries of life. It occurs in this way in esoteric spiritual disciplines like Kabbalah where it is an elaboration of the primary and undeveloped Biblical symbol of the tree of life. This use of the tree as symbol has strong philosophic and universalistic aspects, but it retains the restrictive social quality of being contained in a traditionalized doctrine.

More truly universal, and therefore expressing what is elemental in human existence, are instances of the tree symbol as it is experienced by individuals, in dreams or in the waking events of life, when such experiences are deep enough to bring about a feeling of connection to the inward dimension of reality. A good instance of such an experience that is widely known is that of Brother Lawrence, the seventeenth century Carmelite monk who was a free experimenter in the religious life. He tells of chancing to look at a tree in winter when its branches were bare and of suddenly feeling with tremendous force an intuition of connection with the process of life present in the tree. He felt the rhythm of rebirth at work in nature, and spontaneously he felt it in himself as well. He felt the presence within himself of that same principle of life which would replenish the leaves of the tree in its season, and he recognized that this principle would replenish the barren condition of his life as well. Thus the tree, as a living symbol with a power beyond doctrine, became a psychological instrument of rebirth which Brother Lawrence, in keeping with his background, interpreted in Christian religious terms.

These few instances give an indication of the varieties of forms in which a symbol can appear. We can readily see how large a perspective is necessary if we would appreciate at least some of the diversity of symbolic forms. One observation that cannot fail to be made from our brief review of some aspects of the tree symbol is that each basic symbolic motif may be experienced at successive levels of depth and meaning. From an analytical point of view we may perceive these various levels, mark them off, and describe the details that we see in each aspect of the symbol. But the analysis of symbols does not give us the essence of what is involved. The key is the factor of movement within symbols, the *symbolic unfoldment* that takes place as though spontaneously with the energy coming from an inner momentum that arises from within the symbol itself. The factor of symbolic unfoldment involves the active opening of each symbol as the motif underlying it unfolds and moves from personal to more-than-personal levels within the individual and within the community.

We see expressions of this active factor in all areas of the creative life. It is especially evident in the history of literature, in drama, in poetry, and in novels. The literary use of symbols, when it is validly and successfully carried out, has a way of reaching beyond itself, beyond its literary framework to an encounter with the trans-symbolic dimension of existence. Thus a symbolic event depicted in a novel will be described and enacted within the context of an individual's life, but if it rings true as a symbol within that person's experience, the reality of it will also strike a chord that will resonate with meanings for many others throughout the culture.

We find, further, that when a literary act has been authentic in its conception and execution, it is effective in a still more profound way. It reaches, then, beyond even the level of psychological depth on which culture is contained. It awakens in individuals a sensitivity to the universals of life. It evokes in individuals a sense of meaningful participation in the ongoingness of human life whatever their cultural time and at whatever point they are living in history. These are the literary works that become the classics. Their immortality stems from the fact that they speak with equal force to the depth of persons in all ages and epochs. We recognize among these the epic poetry of Homer, the drama of Sophocles, the poetry of David, Shakespeare and Dante, among others. What they expressed reached to a depth so basic in the human psyche that it stimulates experiences in other human beings beyond the limitations of space and time. This was because the symbols that governed their writings opened progressively from within themselves toward a level at which the recognition could be basic and universal. Their writings were giving individual expression to *Elemental Symbols.*

That is the factor of symbolic unfoldment at work in the history of literature. It is even more strongly expressed in the history of religion. Specifically, the factor of symbolic unfoldment is the depth psychological ground of the religious awareness by which the individual experiences the immediacy of temporal life in the light of eternity. The equivalent of this is true in every religion, relative in each case to the governing symbol that defines its particular vision of truth.

For example, the person who makes his connection with reality in the context of Christianity may have begun in his childhood with a conventional indoctrination into the stated beliefs and ritual observances of that religion. As the Christian symbolism unfolds by means of deepening inner experiences, it gradually becomes strong enough to work autonomously and express a power of its own within the person. Something much greater and more potent than the personal begins to establish itself. At that point the image of the Christ becomes not merely a doctrine that has been taught as a content of belief, but it becomes a living reality that reaches even beyond itself to give a quality of timelessness and universal meaning to the finite, temporal events of life. Having been worked with diligently and with intense commitment, the Christ symbol has *unfolded.* The bud of the symbol has opened and has spread beyond its religious particularity to a depth that transcends doctrine and reaches to the fullness of human existence in its boundlessness and timelessness. Following this principle of Symbolic Unfoldment, we are led to a way of defining, or identifying a Christian, or by parallel application, identifying a person who professes any other specific doctrine or ideology regarding the nature of reality. A Christian person, we can say, is an individual who lives in terms of the symbols of Christianity, specifically, whose life uses the unfoldment of Christian imagery as a vehicle for finding the universals and providing a context in which to understand the timeless in the experience of individual human beings. The equivalent is true of persons within any other religions and ideologies, be it Muhammedanism, Marxism, Judaism, Hinduism, or any other. The symbols that carry our beliefs, whatever they may be, are the vehicles that transport us from the finite events of our lives to the perception of infinity as the context that gives meaning to our individual experiences.

This perspective of the spontaneous power of symbols gives us a framework for understanding the cultural effects when historical events are rehearsed in the form of religious ritual. In Jewish religious practice, for example, the historical events by which the people were redeemed from slavery by Moses and led with great difficulty into a Promised Land is reenacted each year in the observance of the Passover ritual. In this form, as the prayers are read and the story is retold, it becomes fixed in the mind of the child who is participating in it, mainly as an observer, in the largely pleasant ritual of retelling an event of history in the context of a family feast. Listening to the prayers and readings, the child perceives that the historical events are "good" since the present fathers continue in the spirit of the many generations of forefathers in venerating these events. They are felt affirmatively on the inner level of historical symbolism. They are events that are incorporated in the continuity of religious tradition. As long as they remain on this level, they only carry potentials for cultural experience. When the symbol begins to work actively, however, in the consciousness of the social group, carried by the children's learned awareness of historical events in the form of traditions, a process of symbolic unfoldment is set into motion. The experience of the symbol deepens and becomes larger. Increasingly the several levels of profundity that are implicit in the symbols come to the fore and establish themselves. In this case they are specifically the image of bondage in a materialistic and idolatrous land; freedom from slavery achieved with a help and guidance that have a greater-than-natural source; a lengthy period of suffering in the wilderness followed by entry into the Promised Land; the additional Mosaic prophecies that prosperity will make the people forgetful of God, that this will lead to desolation and suffering, which will be followed in due course by repentance and redemption; and finally that this cycle of history will be repeated again and again in the generations to come until the people learn to remember.

It is not too much to say, even where the observance of religious ritual has lapsed, that the psychological support provided by the recurrent telling and the consequent unfolding of this symbol on the inner level of personal experience has made it possible for the Jewish people to survive disaster after disaster for three thousand years, and to emerge even from the Nazi holocaust re-established in the promised land of Israel. Here we see an instance of the factor of symbolic unfoldment manifesting itself on a social level in the midst of history. It is evidence too that when the unfoldment of a major symbol takes place culturally under the pressure of historical events it can give a sacramental quality to those events even in the midst of a secular environment and under the profane conditions of modern commerce and technology.

These religious and historical situations of which we speak are instances of profound symbols being experienced in terms of a social tradition. Often, however, this is not a possibility in modern times. We find ourselves increasingly in situations in which individuals are cut off from the symbols of the past. For varied reasons they have no access to them. At first it seems that such people are cut adrift in life with no spiritual resources on which to draw. Soon, however, it becomes apparent that this alienation from religious traditions presents an unexpected opportunity. These modern individuals are thrown back upon themselves, which is to say, they are forced to bestir the depths that have become dormant in themselves to fill the vacuum left by the old symbols. For them the outcry "God is dead" is not so much a theological pronouncement as a psychological fact. In their inner experience the most basic symbol of the culture has lost its force, and sharp pangs of spiritual hunger are the result.

With such people, deprived of traditional resources, we have to start afresh. Theirs is a difficult and often painful condition, for they can hardly avoid the psychological disturbances that have become endemic to modern man. But out of the chaos through which they must pass—indeed, because of this chaos—there arises the possibility of drawing new and potent symbols out of the depths of alienated individuals, and with these new symbols remaking the image of our time.

In this context the factor of symbolic unfoldment is exceedingly useful, both for its descriptive value in enabling us to understand the dynamics of what is taking place in a person and as a tool for expanding the range of individual consciousness. It provides us with a perspective and with clues to a method for drawing modern individuals through the labyrinth of personal confusion to a connective experience of life.

One primary characteristic of the modern situation is that lasting experiences of meaning can seldom be achieved through the traditional symbols in their dogmatic forms. This is true, although we know that the great religious traditions possess a reservoir of living symbols in which great psychological and spiritual power still inheres. The question is how the modern person can be given access to this power without being either frightened off or entrapped by its doctrinal overlays.

4

History and the Imagery of Utopia

One of the symbols derived from the reservoir of images in western civilization is the image of utopia. As an image of the ideal condition of human existence it has many aspects, as it has appeared in many forms in the past, varying with the point of view dominant at each period of history. In the time when messianic thinking prevailed, the symbolic equivalent of utopia was the belief in *the end of days* and the coming of *the kingdom of God*. It was out of this vision that Christianity was born. In more recent centuries the image of utopia has been perceived more concretely in the secular terms of life in the world. Thus various visions of utopia have been set forth as idealized communities to be created either by the beneficent intelligence of a philosopher-king, or by the struggle of history moving by a Marxian-type logic toward the classless society.

It is certainly correct to say that each society has its characteristic way of reaching toward, or envisioning, utopia. In Western civilization these visions tend to be brought forth by a particular type of individual whom we may call utopian persons. When, for example, a utopian scheme is developed in Western civilization and is set forth in a literary statement as it was by Thomas More, or when it is developed in more

practical terms as a program of communal living as was
done by Robert Owen, it is primarily the work of an individual. Characteristically a utopian scheme in Western civilization is a personal expression. It is the individual's vision of
how life needs to be lived if human existence is to be meaningful and if man is to fulfill the potentials of his life on
earth.

We can only understand the various utopian plans for
idealized communities if we think of them as projections and
as expressions of the individual's own inner experience. They
arise out of the context and continuity of his inward development, out of the frustrations of his personal life, and out of
the symbolic visions of wholeness and meaning that are
brought forth from the depth of the psyche. This is the basic
principle of psychological life that we find everywhere and
that is the process underlying all those phenomena of man
that can be called creative, or developmental, or growth in
any sense of those words.

This fundamental process constitutes the cycle of energy
movement within a human being. It is the basic cycle, and
we see an eloquent illustration of the ambiguity that it gives
to human life in the personal memoir written by Leo Tolstoy
that he called, "*My Confession.*"* Tolstoy describes there how
meaningless life had become to him after he had achieved
his position of eminence in the literary world of Czarist Russia. Though he had attained the fullest social recognition, all
seemed empty for him. He had been born with an abundance both of wealth and literary talent, and consequently
the first part of his life had been easy and rewarding for him.
When he was hardly thirty, he had found himself securely
established as a leading figure in Russian literary circles.
Money, fame, social position, all were his; and with so little

---

*See *The Religious Writings of Leo Tolstoy*, Julian Press, New York, 1960.

effort that the possibilities for expanding them seemed endless.

In the midst of this, when one might suppose that he would be at his happiest, a basic and bothersome question began to arise in his mind. What is the meaning of life even in the midst of all this success? The question persisted and intrigued him. It tantalized him because he could not answer it, and thus it drew him on. "What," Tolstoy asked himself, "if I should be more famous than Gogol, Pushkin, Shakespeare and Moliere—than all the writers in the world—well, and what then?" He put the question to himself and was forced to report, "I could find no reply."*

It recalls the situation that is described in the Biblical book of Ecclesiastes. There the man of supreme wealth and wisdom, the prototype of whom is King Solomon, the man who has tasted all pleasures of the senses and of society, asked finally: What good is it all? What does it profit a man no matter how much he accumulates in worldly things? The answer of Ecclesiastes was first the well-known, "Vanity of vanities, all is vanity" and then it was a call to return to the piety of conventional religion.

In the course of his growth Tolstoy arrived at both of these answers. Then, as his individual experience continued, he went beyond them.

His first response to the question of the meaning of life was that there was no meaning. All is vanity. But this was not a general answer: Tolstoy understood it very specifically. Without being aware of it and without having reflected upon it, Tolstoy had been acting on the assumption that there is a meaning in life. This meaning was the system of values and beliefs held by the upper class in Czarist Russia, particularly those in the literary circle where popular and financial suc-

---

*Ibid., p. 47.

cess were regarded as the highest goal embodying the meaning of life. Tolstoy had accepted this as the ultimate aspiration of his life, but as he held it in his hand he realized that there was no intrinsic value in it. It was then that the question of the meaning of life arose in him. His old implicit faith had revealed itself to him as a vanity. With that gone he felt himself to be left with nothing to guide him. "I felt that the ground on which I stood was crumbling, that there was nothing for me to stand on, that what I had been living for was nothing, that I had no reason for living."*

This feeling of being completely cut off from life, an absolute lack of contact and support, comes to the fore in the experiences of contemporary persons whenever they are called to confront the ultimate facts of their existence. The absence of a secure belief concerning the meaning of life leaves a void in which it seems that life is no longer possible; or, if it is possible, it is not worth the bother. In Tolstoy's case he was brought to a condition in which he felt no relation to the continuity of human existence. It was natural then that he would conclude that the only reasonable thing for him to do was to kill himself, there in the midst of all his worldly success.

The situation in which this negation of life occurs is one of the fundamental forms in which human beings experience anxiety. The brief remark we quoted from Ecclesiastes is in itself an indication that anxiety of this kind negating life is a universal phenomenon not limited to any particular period of history or culture. But it is a malady to which modern man is especially susceptible; and when it appears it eats at the very heart of personality, even endangering life itself.

It placed Tolstoy's life in jeopardy. Once he felt no meaning in his existence, there seemed to be nothing holding him to life. There was now no longer any reason for living. Just

---

*Ibid., p. 48.

the opposite of such a reason, Tolstoy wrote: "Some irresistible force was dragging me onward to escape from life."* It was as though the principle of life which had previously been constructive and affirmative within him had now reversed itself and was working against him. Now, "The idea of suicide came as naturally to me as formerly that of bettering my life."**

It was at this time that Tolstoy hid all ropes from himself, lest he use them to hang himself. At this time also he would not go hunting, lest he turn the rifle upon himself. We see something that is exceedingly instructive here. While he felt cut off from life, he also felt, although very dimly at the beginning, that a connection to life did exist for him, and that he would find it. Even though the life principle had reversed itself within him and had become negative, a process of life affirmation was still at work. He was suffering because he saw no meaning in life; but the root of that suffering was the urge and need for meaning. Eventually, after it had passed through the negative phase of anxiety, that urge toward meaning expressing the principle of life within him would have to fulfill itself. Thus on the depth level of imagery which carries the futuristic quality of the psyche an intimation was given him that he would eventually experience a renewed connection to life. This was an intimation given before the event, but it provided a nonspecific assurance that helped carry him through the trough of the cycle. It gave him hope even while nothing had yet been shown him that would make his hope specific.

Tolstoy hedged himself against suicide and continued to seek an answer to the question of meaning in life by intellectual means. He reasoned this way and that concerning the nature of God, the story of creation, the discoveries of nine-

---

*Ibid., p. 48.
**Ibid., p. 48.

teenth century science, until finally his reason exhausted itself. And in the moment of this exhaustion he realized that it is inherently not within the power of reason, neither his particular reasoning faculties nor of human reason in general, to discover and define the meaning of life. At that point Tolstoy was ready to accept a faith; for only by faith, he now concluded, can a human being believe his life to be worth the bother of living.

This realization, however, was not an answer to his problem; it only restated it in another form. Granted that a strong faith makes life livable, Tolstoy's difficulty began with the fact that there was no particular belief to which he could give his support. What kind of faith would be possible for him?

"I began to understand," Tolstoy reports, "that in the answers given by faith was to be found the deepest source of human wisdom, that I had no reasonable right to reject them on the ground of reason. And that these principal answers alone solved the problems of life . . . I understood this, but that did not make it any easier for me."* The fact, in other words, that his reason was now giving assent to an act of faith of some sort did not bring such an act of faith any closer; it did not even make it any more possible. All that this new intellectual realization achieved, in fact, was to intensify the internal pressure and to build up an even greater tension around the vacuum of meaning which he felt within himself.

How could he find a faith that he would not merely be in favor of believing, but one that he would actually be able to *feel* as a reality? It would be good if he could accept some structured body of doctrine that had been worked out in generations past by an established church; but that would not be a fact for him. He would not feel the reality of such a faith, and so, no matter how much he might try to convince himself rationally that he ought to place his faith there, the per-

---

*Ibid., p. 81.

sistent questions about the validity of his life would not be silenced. After all, he did not raise those questions rationally and deliberately; they raised themselves of their own power out of some non-rational depth of his being. No trick or strategem would silence them. It would have to be something real.

It would also have to be something that he could verify within his own experience. Now he studied "the conception of an infinite God, of the divinity of the soul, of the way in which the affairs of man are related to God, of the unity and reality of the spirit, man's conceptions of moral good and evil."* He studied the traditional answers to the great and ultimate questions about which man has been concerned throughout his spiritual history. But in these answers which, as he said, had been "worked out through the infinite mental labors of mankind"** he found no support. He felt that he had no alternative but to "reject all this labor of the whole human race and venture on working out the problem in my own way alone."†

---

*Ibid., p. 80.
**Ibid., p. 80, 81.
†Ibid., p. 81.

5

The
Individual Way

"In my own way alone." There are egotistic overtones in that phrase, as though here the great literary artist is pitting himself against all the history of mankind. Not so though. At least not any more. In the earlier period of his life when Tolstoy was primarily a novelist, a phrase like that would have been an indication of his egotism as a creative artist. "In my own way alone" would have expressed the writer's desire to be "original," to be an innovator, or at least distinctive in his work. But such an attitude belonged to the day when he was seeking fame; and that desire no longer stirred in him with any strength. It was part of that meaningless life that had brought him to the brink of suicide.

The phrase "in my own way alone" now expressed a new awareness in Tolstoy, the awareness that the question of the meaning of his life could not be answered for him by any other person in all of creation. Only he himself could recognize it. Only he himself could test it, validate it, verify it in the experience of his life and ultimately know it. Only then would it be a livable fact of his existence. If he sought to take over someone else's doctrines and beliefs and state them as the meaning of his life, it might be intellectually satisfying, but it would not be based on the bedrock of his own being. It would not be authentically his, for it would not have been forged out of his own experience. And no one else could do that for him. Not any more than he could do it for anyone else. He might study the experiences and the conclusions of other persons who had searched for the meaning of life to see whether their insights were relevant to his existence. But the testing and the ultimate decision would have to be made by himself alone. That was how it was when the question of suicide had arisen. No other human being's answer or advice affected the question of whether he, Leo Tolstoy, should live. His alone was the finger that would press the trigger; and ultimately his alone was the feeling for life that made the lasting decision to continue to live.

Tolstoy now realized that the responsibility for finding the meaning of his life rested with no one else than himself, if only because the human race is composed of individuals and that each of these individuals is unique. This new realization, however, filled him with terror.

He recognized the necessary aloneness of human beings, but in the midst of this, and perhaps because of this awareness, he found himself drawn toward something that would balance his aloneness. He was reaching out for a connection with something more than his lonely separate self. Something was missing. He was separated from something to which he should have been connected; how, he did not know. In his inevitable aloneness he felt cut off from life and cut off from God. And the quality of this separation was inward emptiness, a restless ache within, accompanied by terrifying pains of longing.

During this time, Tolstoy writes, "my heart was oppressed by a tormenting feeling. This feeling I cannot describe otherwise than as a searching after God."*

"This search after a God was not an act of my reason, but

---

*Ibid., p. 89.

a feeling, and I say this advisedly, because it was opposed to my way of thinking; it came from the heart. It was a feeling of dread, or orphanhood, of isolation amid things all apart from me, and of hope in a help I knew not from whom."*

Tolstoy was in the midst of the world, and yet isolated, an orphan in the universe. We can sense the emotional anguish contained in his saying, "It was a feeling of dread." In this description of his experiences Tolstoy has given us one of the most expressive and revealing statements of existential anxiety recorded in any of the literature. It is especially instructive because his experience enables us to see the "feeling of dread" as part of an ongoing process. We can recognize here that inherently anxiety has a purpose. It moves toward something greater than itself. Thus, as we follow the course of Tolstoy's personal suffering, we perceive a reconstructive psychological process unfolding in the background of his dreadful isolation.

He felt isolated in the midst of things; nothing was meaningful enough to him to connect him to the stream of life. And yet, in the very midst of this sense of separation, he experienced also a feeling of "Hope in a help I knew not from whom." Why should he feel any intimation of hope at all? Unless the hope is inherent in the anxiety. The seed of the answer to the meaning of existence lies within the very feeling that raises the question. The urge behind the asking carries the intuition of ongoing connection to life by which the doors of awareness are opened.

It seems that there is something within the nature of the human being that leads inherently to the feeling of being separated from life. Perhaps it is the fact of existence as individuals. From it, however, having been drawn into the depths of experiencing one's aloneness a person can discover in the actuality of experience the magnitude of the feeling of

---

*Ibid., p. 89.

connection to life that is possible. In the midst of his despair there came to Tolstoy a wisp of a feeling of hope, and with it an intimation that there exists some being or principle to whom he could turn for meaning and support. He thought of the possibility of God, but his intellectual habits still had a strong hold upon him. From his reading of Immanuel Kant he was, as he writes, "well convinced of the impossibility of proving the existence of God."* That would have stopped this line of searching; but unexpectedly, a still older "former habit" took hold of him. It was a habit he had acquired in childhood and had since discarded, the habit of prayer.

Now he prayed, and as he did so he began to feel the possibility that God does exist and that his life might have a meaning after all. Then he began to think about arguments for the proof of God, and he undertook to establish in his own mind a consciousness of the presence of God. He became increasingly hopeful. Soon, however, he realized that while his intellectual ideas about God sounded good, they would not give him realistically the support he required. Tolstoy wrote, "I began to pray to Him whom I sought that He would help me. But the more I prayed, the clearer it became that I was not heard, that there was no one to whom one could turn."**

The test was an objective one. Was he heard when he prayed? And if not, then all the intellectual arguments about the existence of God and the nature of God were irrelevant. The fact of the matter seemed to be that there is no God to whom one can pray for help; and as Tolstoy came to this conclusion he fell again into a black despair.

In the midst of this despair, however, a significant thing happened. He did not pray another intelligent reasonable prayer, but he heard something in him cry out a prayer. It

---

*Ibid., p. 89.
**Ibid., p. 89.

was not really he who prayed it. The prayer prayed itself. It was, in fact, not really a prayer; it was an unpremeditated outcry, "Lord, have mercy on me and save! O Lord, my God, teach me!"*

And Tolstoy adds the comment, "But no one had mercy on me and I felt that my life had come to a standstill."** At least for the moment.

In the great medieval book of spiritual discipline, *The Cloud of Unknowing*, which deals with various psychological procedures for achieving unity with God, the anonymous author speaks of a type of prayer that is very much like Tolstoy's outcry. It is a prayer that is called forth out of the depth of the spirit by the urgency and the desperation of the need. It is not a long, carefully phrased prayer. The person whose house is afire does not deliver a sermon; he shouts, "Help!" and the urgency of his outcry brings assistance. Thus, the author of *The Cloud of Unknowing* says, "Short prayer pierces Heaven." It is heard and answered because of the spontaneous sincerity with which it is drawn forth by a genuine human need.†

Tolstoy's outcry to God seems to have been such a prayer, and in a comparable way it was answered. After he had called out to God, "Teach me!" an illuminating image appeared to him. He saw himself as a fledgling bird dropped from its nest. It was an image of the kind that carries the thinking processes of the psyche forward in a direct, unpremeditated, intuitive way.

As he lay there helpless on the grass, would he cry out? To whom would he cry? Accompanying his vision there came the feeling that his cry would be to his mother, to her who represented help and support in his life; but it did not seem

---

*Ibid., p. 90.
**Ibid., p. 90.
†*The Cloud of Unknowing*, a modern rendering by Ira Progoff. Julian/Dell New York, 1957, 1983.

to be his mother personally who was involved. It was his mother in the transpersonal terms of *mother* as an elemental symbol, *mother* as the generic source of individual life. "I cannot help seeing." Tolstoy recorded after that image, "that someone who loved me brought me into being. Who is that someone? Again the same answer—God. He knows and sees my search, my despair, my struggle. 'He is,' I said to myself. I had only to admit that for an instant to feel the possibility of existing and the joy of it."*

Here was the answer to the short prayer which had indeed pierced heaven. He had asked to be taught, and spontaneously he had been shown his intimate relation to God as a basic condition of being. Where he had previously felt his sense of isolation and orphanhood, he now knew that *God is* and that he himself is derived from God. With this, an inner connection was established, a sustaining one. He could choose to live again.

Once he had rejected suicide for nothing more than the tactical reason that death, if he killed himself, would be irreversible, and that he would not have an opportunity to change his mind. But that was an answer formed on the intellectual level of the mind. It was therefore no more than an opinion, and it might easily be subject to change. Now, however, his reason for rejecting suicide was deeper than reasoning. It was based on the answer to his spontaneous prayer.

What specifically was the nature of the answer to his prayer? It had been a prayer to God, spontaneously given even though at the time he did not consciously feel that he knew God. To say this means that it was a prayer, an outcry of life, that spoke itself without forethought out of the nonconscious depths of the psyche; and the answer to the prayer came upon the same nonconscious level as that upon which

*Tolstoy, p. 90.

the outcry had been made. The answer came not as a thought but as an image, the image of the bird fallen from its nest; and it was by means of that symbol that an inner knowledge was opened to him.

It would be better to say that with the experience of that symbol an inner knowledge had *begun* to be opened to Tolstoy. What began for him then was the awareness that revelations of the spirit of the kind that may be perceived and described as messages of God actually come to us in the form of symbols using the medium of the nonconscious depths. What opened for him with the image of the fallen bird was an intimation of the spiritual significance of the psychological depths of personality. He began to realize how much of God, of prayers and the valid answering of prayers, transpires there. This was a knowledge that became increasingly important to him later with his dreams. That awareness opened to him now, but his image of the bird was also the beginning of another phase of his interior journey.

6

The Dream
of Leo Tolstoy

After the image that answered Tolstoy's prayer, the balance
shifted again. Being convinced now of the existence of God,
he began to concern himself with special conceptions of God.
He thought of the doctrine of the Trinity and of other theological conceptions and arguments. Thinking now in terms
of concepts, however, his attention shifted from the depths of
himself at the imagery level to the intellectual surface of the
mind. Then, all at once the progress he had made seemed to
disappear. "It melted from before my eyes, as ice melts."* He
fell back into his feeling of emptiness and despair. It seems
that he had reached a sense of relation to God as a basic
condition of being, as an elemental fact of existence beyond
any special doctrine; but when he turned to translate this
experience into the terms of traditional and doctrinal symbolism, it disappeared. It melted away because, as an experience of the fact of being, its essence was beyond doctrine,
and it could not be put into doctrinal form. The net effect
was that having taken a major step forward in the strivings
of his spirit, Tolstoy was once again precariously balanced on
the slim ledge between life and nothingness.

---

*Ibid., p. 90.

He seemed to be back at the point where he started. In this connection, however, Tolstoy made a remark that is of the greatest significance for understanding the cyclic process as it is involved in the spiritual growth of an individual. "Not twice, not three times, but tens, hundreds, of times did I pass through these alternations—now of joy and excitement, now of despair and of consciousness of the impossibility of life."[*]

The testimony of numerous historic persons of the stature of Tolstoy confirm this pattern, and so also does the experience of many modern individuals who have followed the psychological way to interior growth. It is seldom a path of straight direct ascent. Indeed, when it is tranquil and well regulated, the process of growth tends not to deepen and extend itself. Only when a new tension arises are the energies of the psyche stirred again; and out of the intensity of the turmoil a new and larger contact is brought about.

There are substantial psychological reasons why this is so, and they are validated by the reports of individual experience drawn from all the major religious traditions. Perhaps it is to be understood on as elemental a level as the fact that, when one wants to go from one mountain top to the next mountain top, one cannot step lightly from one to the other as the legendary Siegfried did. It is necessary rather to go down into the valley before a new ascent can begin. There is a quality of cyclic rhythm in this that is found throughout the cosmos and is present in the lives of human beings as well. We observe that the spiritual development of persons seldom has the quality of pleasant serenity and certitude that we might idyllically wish. It comes rather in the midst of a continuing struggle, accompanied often by a recurrent tension, the very intensity of which is necessary in order to drive the life energies into the depths of being where fresh contacts and realizations of meaning are to be gained.

---

[*]*Ibid.*, p. 90.

This interior struggle continued in the life of Tolstoy, bringing with it ever new sufferings and awakening ever larger insights and spiritual capacities. At one point the process was crystallized in a long and exceedingly deep dream, the type of dream that serves as a window into the life, consolidating the events of the past and giving a key to the future. Such a dream provides a window through which we can look in two directions. We can look inward through it into the depths of the person to observe the struggles and tensions taking place there. We can also look through it into the future to see in advance the path along which the development of the individual can proceed; usually, indeed, this is a path on which the movement has already begun. A large, life-encompassing dream like this merits close attention, particularly because of the interior light it sheds on the development of a major historic personality; and also because of the perspective it provides for understanding the nature of dreams and the process of personal growth as a whole.

In the dream, Tolstoy writes, "I see myself lying in bed, and I feel neither particularly well and comfortable, nor the contrary. I am lying on my back. I began to think whether it is well for me to lie, and something makes me feel uncomfortable in the legs; if the bed be too short or ill-made, I know not, but something is not right. I move my legs about, and at the same time begin to think how and on what I am lying, a thing which previously had never troubled me. I examine my bed, and see that I am lying on a network of cords fashioned on the sides of the bedstead. My heels lie on one of these cords, my legs on another, and this is uncomfortable. I am somehow aware that the cords can be moved, and with my legs I push the cord away, and it seems to me that thus it will be easier.

"But I had pushed the cord too far; I tried to catch it with my legs, but this movement causes another cord to slip from under me, and my legs hang down. I move my body to get it right again, convinced that it will be easy, but this movement causes other cords to slip and change their places beneath me, and I perceive that my position is altogether worse; my whole body sinks and hangs, without my legs touching the ground. I hold myself up only by the upper part of the back, and I feel now not only discomfort, but horror. I now begin to ask myself what I had not thought of before. I ask myself where I am, and on what I am lying. I begin to look around, and first I look below, to the place toward which my body sank, and where I feel it must soon fall. I look below, and I cannot believe my eyes.

"I am on a height far above that of the highest tower or mountain, a height beyond all my previous powers of conception. I cannot even make out whether I see anything or not below me, in the depths of that bottomless abyss over which I am hanging, and into which I feel drawn. My heart ceases to beat, and horror fills my mind. To look down is horrible. I feel that if I look down I shall slip from the last cord, and perish. I stop looking, but not to look is still worse, for then I think of what will at once happen to me when the last cord breaks. I feel that I am losing, in my terror, the last remnant of my strength, and that my back is gradually sinking lower and lower. Another instant, and I shall fall.

"Then all at once comes into my mind the thought that this cannot be true—it is a dream—I will awake.

"I strive to wake myself, and cannot. 'What can I do? What can I do?' I ask myself, and as I put the question I look above.

"Above stretches another gulf. I look into this abyss of heaven, and try to forget the abyss below, and I do actually forget it. The infinite depth repels and horrifies me; the infinite height attracts and satisfies me. I still hang on the last cords which have not yet slipped from under me, over the abyss; I know that I am hanging thus, but I look only upwards, and my terror leaves me. As happens in dreams, I hear a voice saying, 'Look well; it is there!' My eyes pierce farther and farther into the infinity above, and I feel that it calms me. I remember all that has happened, and I remember how it happened—how I moved my legs, how I was left hanging in the air, how I was horrified, and how I was saved from my horror by looking above. I ask myself, 'And now, am I not hanging still?' and I feel in all my limbs, without looking, the support by which I am held. I perceive that I no longer hang, and that I do not fall, but have a fast hold. I question myself how it is that I hold on. I touch myself, I look around, and I see that under the middle of my body there passes a stay, and looking up I find that I am lying perfectly balanced, and that it was this stay alone that held me up before.

"As happens in dreams, the mechanism by which I am supported appears perfectly natural to me, a thing to be easily understood, and not to be doubted, although this mechanism has no apparent sense when I am awake. In my sleep I was even astonished that I had not understood this before. At my bedside stands a pillar, the solidity of which is beyond doubt, though there is nothing for it to stand on. From this pillar runs a cord, somehow cunningly and at the same time simply fixed, and if I lie across this cord and look upward, there cannot be even a question of my falling. All this was clear to me, and I was glad and easy in my mind. It seemed as if someone said to me, 'See that you remember!'"*

Tolstoy closes his Confessions by telling us this dream. He adds no remarks about it and attempts no interpretation. He seems to feel that its meaning is transparent and easy to perceive, especially in the light of the experiences he has been describing. In fact, far from believing that dreams are dark and difficult to understand, Tolstoy tells this dream in order to help his reader see more clearly by means of the dream

---

Ibid., pp. 107–109

symbolism the things he has been trying to describe in his direct literary way. "This dream," he says, "repeated for me in a condensed form all that I had lived through and described, and I therefore think that a description of it may . . . serve to render clearer, to refresh the remembrance of and to collect into one whole, all that has been described."*

Tolstoy seems to have recognized intuitively one of the primary traits of dreams which the observations of depth psychology have uncovered. This is the *recapitulative time quality* of dreams. At each present moment in which a dream occurs, there is a tension of time. This is a tension between the future that is trying to bring itself into existence, and the past that clings, as by a force of psychological gravity, to whatever has already been established. The impulse of the past is to resist change, just as this impulse of the future is to seek to bring it about. Out of this impasse, when the pressure becomes strong enough, the process of dreaming is stimulated at a deep level. It is then that large, recapitulative dreams are brought about.

In these dreams the energies of the life move back over the past and draw up the quintessence of what has transpired in the person's life, restating it in relation to the crisis of the present moment. The dream is selective as it chooses and restructures those aspects of the past that are relevant for the present. It does this in symbolic forms, using a series of images that are the equivalent of trenchant and pithy phrases in the power of their expressiveness. Deep dreams are the spontaneous poetry of the human personality because of the natural imaginativeness of their symbolism. These symbols in their concise recapitulations have the effect of carrying forward the developmental process at the depth of the person. They restate the past in such a form that it inadvertently opens a path by which the life of the person can

---

Ibid., p. 106

move beyond the impasses of the present into the future. In this way a new, personal perspective emerges, evoked by the tensions within the life of the person and carried from the past into the future in symbolic forms by the deep recapitulative dreams.

What is brought about then is not an intellectual perspective perceived and felt upon the depth level of imagery. We should realize that the overall goal in this process reaches much beyond dreaming. Essentially, the life of the person is seeking to move out of the situation in which it has been stymied by first drawing back in order to gain greater momentum for another attempt by a forward thrust (Reculer pour mieux sauter). Thus it begins by moving back in time and then moving forward again. Dreams are a particularly felicitous instrument for assisting this process of movement at the depth of a person's life. Their aptness and brevity make it possible to compress and describe the relevant elements of the past in an economical and efficient form. On this base the recapitulative quality of dreams then can carry the growth of the life forward as a natural, spontaneous process because of the tension of time out of which it is born. Tolstoy's dream is an excellent instance of this. We can learn much from examining it closely.

In the dream Tolstoy found himself lying in bed, feeling that something was not as it should be. He could not tell specifically what was wrong, only that something in general seemed to be amiss. His legs were not comfortable. Perhaps the bed was too short or was broken somewhere. He could not tell what it was, but something definitely was wrong. This starting point of the dream seems to be identified with the earlier situation of his life. He had been successful in the literary world and in society with many comforts and pleasures in his life, and yet something had not been as it should be. In his life as in his dream he could not say specifically what the trouble was, only that something was out of kilter.

Something was not right. It had to do with the way he took himself around in the world. His legs were not comfortable.

Up to that time he had taken things for granted. He had not asked questions about the validity of what he was doing. But now, feeling uncomfortble, he found himself asking questions. Was his behavior good? Or was it evil? What was the meaning of his way of life? Is there any more valid meaning of life to which he could turn for guidance?

Tolstoy found himself asking these questions in his daily life. In the dream this was represented by his looking around at his bed to see what he was lying on. It was not at all what he had expected. He had been assuming that he was lying on a substantial bed with posts and a mattress that would hold his weight securely. But now he perceived that his bed was nothing more than a network of cords. It was a very flimsy thing, delicate and most insubstantial. He realized that he was not only uncomfortable but that he was actually in a precarious situation.

At this point, however, he still thought that it was not really a serious matter; a small change, a slight readjustment, and everything would be all right again. To accomplish this he moved the cord slightly, just a little bit, but that little bit was too much, and all at once everything was altogether out of balance.

Here Tolstoy's experience followed a fundamental human pattern. When something basic is wrong in a person's life, the way it first reveals itself is in some small thing that seems as though it can easily be remedied. A little fixing will quickly do it. But in the act of fixing it the covering is moved, and then one realizes the gaping hole that is underneath. There is a hole that had always presented a great danger, but it was a danger that had been ignored because it had not been seen.

In his dream Tolstoy saw the precarious situation just as he saw it in his life when he began to seek a valid meaning for his activities in the world. He looked around himself to see how things were lying. He looked at the bed and at his position on it, and he realized that things were actually a great deal worse than he had expected. His body was sinking, and he was being held up only by a part of his back. Now he was not only uncomfortable but horrified. It was time now to ask still more fundamental questions, not only about the bed he was lying on—that is to say, not only about the situation of his own life—but about the underlying condition of man's existence. Where was he? What was he doing here?

At that point the dream represented the intense anxiety, the dreadful aloneness and unsafeness he had felt. He was at a height beyond the highest mountain, so high that he could see nothing at all below. He was, in other words, completely out of touch with the foundations of his existence. This position in the dream is a characteristic, in many ways a classic representation, of the underlying anxiety of modern man. Being so high up in his world of intellect and culture, modern man has no connection with the ground of life on which he must walk in the world. No wonder he feels insecure; no wonder his legs feel uncomfortable. We find very similar themes and symbolisms among the dreams of modern persons, especially in our present generation.

Tolstoy saw himself in the dream as being at an incalcuable height. He was so high up he could not measure or even conceive it. And he was perched there most precariously; all that was holding him was a thread, one single cord. And below him was a bottomless abyss, so deep he could not see the end of it. If the last cord should slip! He dared not think of it. He could not bear to look at it, for the abyss below him seemed to be drawing him into it. No wonder, as Tolstoy tells us. "My heart ceases to beat, and horror fills my mind."* But in the very midst of this dreadful tension, his situation became clearer.

---

*Ibid., p. 107

While he felt this horror and was virtually paralyzed by it, something elemental in him understood the specific possibilities before him. If he looked downward and saw the bottomless abyss, he would be drawn into it; in that instant a decision was implicitly made within Tolstoy. He decided that he would resist looking down. The alternative, however, seems to have been even worse. If he did not look down into the abyss he would think about what would happen to him when he fell into it; and that would be dreadful beyond all conception. The involuntary thinking was the great danger, and he realized that he was not capable of controlling his thoughts. Tolstoy sensed that it was this lack of control that would finally destroy him, if it did not regulate itself. He felt himself to be losing strength and slipping away. At this point, the dream corresponded to the situation in his life during the time when he feared he might not be able to prevent himself from taking his own life.

Now there came a last desperate effort to dismiss the whole thing as though it were nothing at all. All this terror he felt within the dream, why it is only a bad joke. It is nothing more than a bad dream, he said to himself; when I awaken it will be over and forgotten. I shall laugh at it and go about my old accustomed happy ways.

In that aspect of the dream it was the conventional social self of Tolstoy that was speaking, expressing the old, environmental side of his personality. This was indeed the attitude that had dominated his life in the past. It was the side of him that valued his high social position, that administered his estates with financial care, that courted favor in literary circles, and maintained his family as a social institution. It was this side of him that appeared in the dream as a voice that was saying to him, "This search for meaning is a foolish diversion. Go back to work. Write your novels; manage your property; see that your finances grow." And that is exactly the attitude that his wife and his old friends took toward his quest for meaning in life. They personified in the outer world the old environmental attitude that had dominated his life, and an environmental voice corresponding to them expressed it in the dream. In many forms and repeatedly they had been saying to him during his time of crisis, "Come out of your dream and get back to reality." But where was reality to be found?

The tension and the terror had become so horrifying to him that he was ready to capitulate. He would go back and become conventionally good and conforming. But now that he wanted to would he be able to get out of the dream? No, he could not. There was no way out of the dream, for the dream was the reality of his life.

This is what the dream was telling him. There was no place else to go. This was his life situation, and it represented the human life situation as well. With all its terror, that is what it is. Try as one will, one cannot escape from it. Therefore relax in it; accept it, and be in it. For, the dream is saying, though life may seem to be but a dream, this dream is your reality.

As in the dream, so in life, we cannot get out of it. We are there, in the midst of it, and by the very nature of things, we have no place else to turn. But this realization that there is no escape, no exit, seems to reverse the entire situation. The truly central awakening is to the fact that there is no other place to which one can go, and no other place to which one can fall; thus there need be no fear. Why then the terror, and the depth and intensity of the dream of falling? Because, it would seem, the terror is inherent in the situation; and when the terror is experienced, a doorway is opened to a more profound awareness of the total situation of life. In the act of continous falling into the bottomless abyss, the realization comes that, for all the movement and the fear, there is no other place to which one can fall. There is no bottom on which one can be injured. It is a groundless fear, just as it is a groundless abyss. The faller, the falling, and the abyss all are one.

When a person tries to awaken from a terrifying dream such as Tolstoy's and finds that he cannot, the first sensation is of great horror; for he feels that he is caught without a means of escape. But the second feeling is of a reawakening to life. In the moment when he realizes that he cannot escape, he knows also that this is really where he belongs. He belongs there in the dream, for the dream is reality. He is in the right place after all. The paradox of anxiety and existence opens from within, and a new awareness of connection to life begins.

It was so in the dream when Tolstoy tried to awaken himself and could not. He called out, "What can I do?" And this calling out was another instance of those spontaneous "short prayers that pierce heaven." In the dream, at the very instant when his cry came forth, he found his attention drawn above in a way that quieted and sustained him. A new supporting connection had been achieved. Somehow it had been effected, but not by his conscious doing. Now he looked up into a great gulf of heaven, felt himself drawn to it, and he was able actually to forget the fearsome abyss he had seen below. This forgetting was also an overcoming of major proportions. It represented a great psychological victory. It meant that his thoughts were coming under control so that he would be able to look upward steadfastly. He would be able to keep his life focussed toward a still undisclosed purpose; that is, he would be able to continue looking upward. And as long as he looked upward, the dream told him, all would be well. "I still hang on the last cords which have not yet slipped from under me, over the abyss; I know that I am hanging thus, but I look only upwards, and my terror leaves me."*

It was with a new realization of the quality of his support

---

*Ibid., p. 108.

in life that Tolstoy looked up into the infinity above him. He
had a completely new way to experience and interpret all
that had happened to him. He turned to this now in the
dream and in the perspective of his new awareness he considered afresh the events that had taken place. The past of his
life now took on a new meaning in the perspective of a
freshly opening future. "I remember all that has happened,
and I remember how it happened—how I moved my legs,
how I was left hanging in the air, how I was horrified and
how I was saved from my horror by looking above."* Now at
last he was able to realize that he was no longer hanging
precariously, but that he did have a fast hold. And what was
it that was holding him so securely? A single stay under the
middle of his body on which he was lying perfectly balanced.

Tolstoy remarks that when he awoke, this apparatus that
held him up seemed inconceivable. It was much too slim to
have been able to bear his weight. In the dream, however,
there was no question about it. He felt himself to be held
securely, even though it was on a slim and insubstantial
cord. It was, to be sure, a precarious security, in that its physical supports were meagre; but the sense of the dream was
that this would be more than adequate. This was perhaps
the dream's way of saying that his life was sustained not by
physical supports, but by supports of quite another kind; for
this, just as the reference to "up" and "down" in the dream,
was to be taken symbolically.

Tolstoy's life was balanced on a slim cord, and yet, he
felt, "there cannot be even a question of my falling." The
inner sense of the dream carried a certitude that was not to
be doubted. Often this kind of insight that comes in a dream,
the knowledge that without specific evidence something is
"just so," is the most important. It is as though the depths of
the person are expressing an awareness that is so elemental,

Ibid., p. 108.

so basic, that even the dream process cannot find a visual symbol adequate to represent it. The knowledge given him is direct and strong. He cannot fall. No matter how thin the cord that holds him, he is securely held. "See that you remember," the voice said, to underscore the importance and the validity of this new knowledge. And apparently Tolstoy was so impressed by the dream that he did remember it. He noted it carefully and returned to it again and again in the years that followed, recalling it as a major turning point in his life.

7

The Inner Process of
a Utopian Person

The record of Tolstoy's life in the years that followed his dream indicates that he did retain the insight it had brought him. But the same record indicates that he also forgot it on many occasions. At those times he was once again out of touch with life, lost and confused. It was as though the dream and the enlarged awareness that it carried had never happened to him, as though they had never been part of his life. The insights were unremembered then. All that he had learned had to be discovered anew, not once but ten, a hundred times more, as he had already observed of his experiences in his *Confessions* before the dream appeared. The dream had opened a door for him into a room which he desperately needed to enter, but many times afterward he inadvertently wandered out of that room, lost his way, and could get back in again only with the greatest difficulty.

After that dream, Tolstoy lived thirty active years until his death at the age of eighty two. During those years he experienced the extremes of wonderful liberating awareness together with bitter and dark depressions. In one sense the dream had come to him as a blessing, as a symbolic entry to a new level of experience; in another sense it contained a record of the spiritual struggle through which he had lived, and it was also a harbinger of more struggle to come. It was the sign of a blessing that could be fulfilled only with a strong and repeated intermixture of suffering. All of his life seemed to reflect the same paradox that was involved in his urges to suicide. The pain and the despair were present throughout, as though a purposeful image were in the background of the whole process. Even while his inner energies were moving downward and away from the world, he felt the intimation of a meaning unfolding which would no longer permit him to be merely an orphan in the universe.

This image, or intimation, of what the final outcome of the cylical inner process would be was present inherently through the process as a whole. It was there as the meaning and as the implicit goal of it, even while the process was in its negative phase. It carried an intimation of meaning, the goal of which was life, even while the life energies were in the darkness and were working against themselves. It was there as the tulip is buried beneath the ground, present as the goal and as the effective principle in the bulb, even during the time when no sign of growth has yet appeared on the surface.

The experience of meaning and of connection to life was implicit in the process through all its dark phases, for this was the image behind it. We can see in this one of the essential characteristics of hope, that hope establishes itself in the midst of hopelessness and that hope both discovers itself and affirms itself by means of the experience of hopelessness into which it falls.

It is the absence of hope that makes hope necessary and that sets into motion the process by which it is eventually firmly established. When we possess hope, and when it possesses us, coloring our perceptions of life with optimism and enthusiasm, we tend to take hope for granted. At such times we do not think about it. When hope is gone, however, when no supportive connection to life is felt, the inner life is

thrown into disorder. By means of this disorder an integrative image is activated and brought into the person's life.
It is a cyclic process. Out of the confusion and interior turmoil comes a further image, often expressed in a general
movement of imagery. Whatever its specific content, it is an
image that contains the potentials for the next step in the
person's life. The image carries the energies of hope. But it is
not hope that is focused toward any specific object of desire.
Thus it is not limited. It is hope that expresses the movement
of life itself. At that point, before hope has been limited by
being stated in terms of preconceived conscious desires, hope
carries the energies of pure potentiality. The ground of hope
is then a person's intuitive realization of being connected to
life by the very nature of existence. This connection can then
unfold out of the imagery depths within the person.

In this context we can see that the hopelessness of Tolstoy
was psychologically essential and eventually became a constructive factor. When he had gone the furthest away from
the world and the deepest into the darkness, the darkness
itself was stirred to light. But this is no mere metaphor. It is a
key to the dynamic underlying the dialectical process of the
psyche. Images that are submerged and dormant in the
depths of the person are awakened when the energies have
been drawn far enough down with sufficient force and intensity. The awakening of these images has the effect of bringing about a new realization of meaning, for it establishes a
new point of contact with life. The vehicle for this new connection is an image whose quality is other than personal.
This is the crux of it. The tension is brought about by difficulties on the personal level of life, or what is sometimes called
the interpersonal level, where there is a confusion and a conflict in the individual's relation to his environment, to the
wishes of other persons. This was Tolstoy's problem. At one
point, as he writes in his diaries, he could not feel the reality
of the self of another person. He could not feel the reality of

what Buber has called the Thou. But later this awareness was given to him very strongly and very meaningfully.

In Tolstoy's situation the emotional disturbance which eventually had a creative effect began as an intensely felt personal problem. It turned his energies inward and downward in regression until they touched and awakened elemental images of a larger than personal scope. It was these symbols that provided the medium for a contact with reality beyond any of his previous personal perspectives or concerns. This was the significance to him of the voice telling him that if he would look upward steadfastly all would be well.

When such an image is awakened, it may be brought to the fore in a dream, in a waking image, or in a life-event that contains the elements of a connective experience. Eventually its effect will be unifying and integrative, but its first phases will be symbolic and promissory. It will be pointing toward a movement of events that hold possibilities for the future, but it is referring to these possibilities before they are fulfilled. In that sense it is promissory. It is giving the person an intimation of things to come; or, better said, an intimation of things that are possible. The dream that we have discussed opened a door for Tolstoy personally at that time, but it was necessary for him to have many more experiences in various forms over a period of several years before the promise of that dream could become clear to him and could begin to be fulfilled in his life. Gradually as the outcome of numerous encounters in his life, Tolstoy came to a point of realizing how the intangible principle of non-violence and love can be expressed as a power working in the world. This became the connective and integrative factor in his life during his later years.

In the life of Tolstoy these continuing experiences had a transformative effect on two levels. On the one hand they brought him a new vision that gave a recreative meaning to his personal existence. Further than that, they established a point of contact within him that enabled him to open a new channel of non-violent power in history. It seems, and this remark must be added, that for several reasons, this experience of inward contact was not strong enough in Tolstoy himself to have an effect in history within its own terms. But it did continue and extend itself in a person like Gandhi, and in other persons of comparable inner experience. The result is that the principle of non-violence that was formed in Tolstoy in the midst of the painful cycles of his inner life may yet become an important spiritual factor in history, even in the technological civilization of the present day.

The point to bear in mind is that it is only when the level of experience has been markedly shifted from the surface to the depth that experiences of transpersonal meaning and transpersonal effect become possible. The misleading factor, however, is that the forms in which these experiences are expressed tend not to be directly literal. Coming from a depth in the person, they are symbolic, often unclear since they are distant, or seemingly foreign, to the immediate environment, and they are promissory in the sense that they come ahead of time, ahead of the actuality of events. Thinking of this dream of Tolstoy, and also of the cyclic experiences within his life, we also think of the Prophets, especially Ezekiel. We realize that the outwardly strange symbolic experiences of the Prophets could carry their special awareness and power only because of the depth and distance within the person from which they came. The obscurity and strange (to outward frames of reference) symbolic style are inherently connected to the depth and power and validity of the visions. There could not be one without the other.

The dialectical aspect of the imagery process is apparent, for the opposites are there together. We note also that when experiences take place at the elemental depths of the person they are not limited to the individual in whom they occur. When elemental and transpersonal symbols have been touched and aroused, by whatever personal disturbance or situation, these symbols behave as though they have a life of their own. It is as though there is a guiding and directive principle working within them and through them. They seem to be able to reach and extend themselves along a dimension that has no walls, moving from person to person as suits their transpersonal need, and using individuals as instruments toward an unfolding purpose.

These are characteristics of the kind of human being whom we have called the Utopian Person. I have chosen to speak about Leo Tolstoy at some length primarily because his personality and life express many of the characteristics of that type of person as it appears in Western civilization. This is especially true because of the difficulties he encountered, for it enables us to see how profoundly the experience of anxiety is related to the appearance of a vision of meaning and hope.

Taking Tolstoy as our focus of study, we can think of the Utopian Person as having three main characteristics, to which a fourth must ultimately be added. These are: 1) the intense individuality of his experience; 2) the universality of it; 3) the personal need for social application; 4) the integrative quality of his experiences and their unifying effect upon his personality.

1. The intense individuality that characterized Tolstoy's experience. He was intensely involved in his personal life, and it seems even that he drew from the tensions of his personal conflicts and the disturbances they brought about, the force with which to deepen his search. This is how it must be, for the intense concern to find a personal meaning in life is what sends the energies into the depths and makes a transformative experience possible.

A first characteristic of the Utopian Person, however, is that he is so constituted that he cannot rest or be content with any solution to his personal conflicts that does not involve also an enlarging and integrative experience of transpersonal meaning in his life. Because of this stringent requirement, the tension builds, sometimes causing the tremendous disturbance that looks like schizophrenia, and finally leads to the unifying awareness that it requires.

2. The second characteristic of the Utopian Person is that, beginning with intense individuality, he comes finally to establish a relation with himself that is cast in universal terms. He thinks of himself then less as an individual than as a human being. The meaning of his existence and the power of his personal being are felt precisely in the fact that the pressure of his personal psyche has led him to a point where he can live beyond purely personal requirements.

3. The third characteristic of the Utopian Person is that having touched the universal in himself, and having transmuted his personal existence by means of it, he cannot rest content until the image that has come to him has been made meaningful and applicable for the fellowmen who live in his community or nation. The image of life that was first sought because of a personal need is found finally on a transpersonal level. And the full search is not completed until that image has been brought into a form in which it can be lived, not only by the Utopian Person himself but by his fellowmen as well.

This is the pattern that underlies the behavior of all reformers. It expresses a prophetic quality, and it is the image of the prophet that is the closest to the Utopian Person. The distinction to be noted between the social political reformer on the one hand and the Utopian Person on the other lies in the depth at which their guiding and transforming experience is reached. When it is on the level of intellectual doctrine or political tactics, this is the social style of the reformer. But when the guiding experience has touched the bases of life and is felt as an embodiment of ultimate principle in the world translated into social terms so that the incursion of the transpersonal can be shared equally among all men, this is the image of the Prophet at work, and we can then speak of a Utopian Person.

4. The fourth characteristic of the Utopian Person involves the fact that all three of these aspects are characteristically experienced by him as a unity. His personal life, his contact with the transpersonal, and his relationship to his fellowman are all one. But the hallmark of his life is that he begins by being fragmented, and this is shown in the fact that he begins by being caught in conflict and in maladaptation in each of these three categories. The intensity of his difficulties leads to disturbances which extend all through the psyche, and finally bring about the pressure that makes a new integrative vision not only possible but necessary.

When that vision comes, it draws the psyche together and places a single directive principle at the core of the individual's life. His inward life and his outward life then become one. His personal life and his social life become one. The meaning of his existence as an individual human being is not felt to be separate from the existence of other human beings. From the point of view of psychopathology this is a lack of capacity to differentiate; but from another point of view, it is the capacity to enter the connective dimension of human existence where I and Thou become one as a fact of experience, and where it becomes possible to so restructure and rededicate one's life that a larger-than-personal factor expresses itself in one's affairs.

8

The Dialectic
of Hope and Anxiety

A main characteristic of the Utopian Person is that he or she is a type of individual whose inward needs can be fulfilled only through a vision that reaches outward and goes beyond subjective experience. He needs to feel that he can embody this vision in the world so that it is a feasible goal toward which he can work in his life. In this sense the Utopian Person is the social prototype of the process of life-integration as a whole. Not that Utopian Persons necessarily achieve a large measure of harmony in their lives; the main indications are indeed to the contrary, if we can judge from the lives of persons like Tolstoy. Their lives are spent in a quest to achieve in actuality something of which they know only by intuition. They have glimpsed it only as a possibility in the form of an image; and yet they feel the social need to explain it to those who are around them. Thus they are subject to a double pressure, from within themselves and from persons outside of them. And the pressures are increased by their own unsureness. Nonetheless the Utopian Person has the need to fulfill the image in whatever way and to whatever degree is possible. In the midst of contention on the outer level of life, therefore, the image experienced in the depth of the Utopian Person is often expressed in an artwork that is felt as being very private and personal, but is also much more than personal.

The pressure felt by the Utopian Person is both inward and outward simultaneously. On the one hand the energies move into inward depths seeking truths that are transpersonally valid; at the same time these energies press outward to express these truths in social situations that will make them tangible and livable for other human beings. The nature of the Utopian Person is such that he cannot be content until he has brought about an outward expression of his inward ideal, until the personal vision has been converted into social reality. He lives therefore in the midst of a tension of opposites, a tension of inward and outward; and this tension can only find release when it is embodied in a social doctrine or a social program that can be presented to the community. This becomes the *opus* of the Utopian Personality, the *artwork* that embodies in outward life the need and vision of inward life. The *opus* thus provides the field in which the psychological tensions are resolved integrally by uniting the opposing forces of the psyche.

This tendency and drive in the Utopian Person expresses an underlying principle of the functioning of the psyche. The psyche works progressively toward the resolution of inner conflict by projecting the elements of the conflict into an opus in which they can be integrated and given a new form. A constructive dialectic is at work in this process. In Hegel's terms we see it in the fact that, when the *thesis* of the inward drive meets the *antithesis* of the outward pressure, the resulting conflict leads to the emergence of a new *synthesis*. The complications that arise are in the steps that intervene between the conflict of thesis and antithesis and the emergence of the synthesis as the opus of the life. These are difficulties that are essentially of a psychological nature, but they especially involve the phenomenology of time in the dialectic of the psyche. In the case of the Utopian Person, it has two aspects that must be studied. One involves the tension of time in the individual psyche; the other, the cultural complications that result when an individual psyche projects itself into the arena of history.

As we retrace the sequence of events in the psyche of the Utopian Person, we come first to the condition of impasse that is the crisis of his life. It is here, where he confronts the meaninglessness of existence, that creative experience begins. The life energies are unable at that point to find a satisfying channel of expression in the outer world, and so they turn inward. They are forced to go ever deeper into the psyche until they touch and awaken there some large but dormant image, an elemental symbol that brings to the person a new vision of the possibilities of life. This vision is personal, and it opens for the individual who experiences it a connection to the inner principle of meaning in human existence. It provides a new context that makes life significant and livable for him as, for example, such an experience did for Leo Tolstoy. When, however, he takes the next necessary step of giving social form to his vision an important change takes place.

If the symbol that opens for him is of fundamental meaning, if it carries a vision of the social or political nature of man, the desire will necessarily be to communicate it. The need of the Utopian Person is to give the utopian image expression. To do this it is necessary to articulate the specific image of utopia, to develop it in terms of concepts that can be communicated, and to support it with a logical structure of argument. When this has been done, however, the symbolic vision is transformed. It is no longer a fluid expression of the movement of life. It has become a doctrine.

Likewise, if the vision takes the forms of a social program, it becomes a rallying point to the degree that it succeeds in the world. Allegiance is given to it, and in time it becomes an orthodoxy. The Utopian vision becomes a fixed goal, and when this happens, it is cut off from the flow of inward experience that was its source.

This is the process of hardening that is inherent in the visionary hopes of man. Solidification begins as soon as the inward is made concrete in an outward form. Then the hope that the vision embodied is no longer a flowing affirmation of life. In going outward it narrows itself. The hope becomes a definite goal; and when this happens, its free connection with the unfoldment of life is closed off.

In moving outward it goes into its opposite. The *thesis* of hope becomes the *antithesis* of anxiety. Both of these opposites are necessary, and they must be both understood and lived through before the synthesis of the opus can be achieved.

In the Utopian Person to whom the symbolic vision comes, hope is the expression of the affirmation of life that accompanies his experience. In the intensity of his struggle, he sought an answer; and when that answer was disclosed to him in the depth of himself, a burst of energy that under-scored the resilience and resourcefulness of the processes in-herent in the psyche came with it. Then with all the depths of his being he could believe in life. Hope was given to him, and this was not limited to hope for anything in particular. It was a hope addressed to the full potentiality of life becoming manifest in all the forms of human existence. It was in this sense that the Psalmist could say, "My hope is in the Lord." The hope he placed in the Lord did not set restrictions on what God should do. The Psalmist did not specify what he hoped for. He simply affirmed his faith in the power of life and in its abundance.

The fullness of hope is expressed in this, hope that is un-conditioned by restrictions on what is hoped for. In contrast to this, when hope is projected outward and is concretized in a specific goal, a different context is set up in the psyche. Its focus then is on the outer object or goal, and to that degree it is no longer an expression of faith in the pure process of life, which is the *Lord* of the Psalmist. When this has taken place, we are no longer entitled to speak psychologically of hope, for the psychological condition that has then been established is not hope as the affirmation of life, but it is *desire*. It is desire because it is now directed toward particular objectives, the conceptions of which have been formed by the past experience of the individual.

When hope becomes desire, the psychological situation of the personality is fundamentally transformed. A totally different set of dynamics is set in operation, principally because a new quality of tension is established in the psyche. This tension expresses the fact that the experience of time is narrowed. When hope is experienced as an unconditioned affirmation of life there is an open relation to the unfolding possibilities of existence. The future is uninhibited. But when hope has become desire, the future can unfold only in the shadow of the past. The movement of the psyche can only follow the patterns that have been developed before. The trends of behavior, since they have been established in the past, tend to work toward goals that have not had an opportunity for the emerging future to place its stamp upon them.

A curious ambiguity of time thus covers those goals that are objects of desire. As goals of behavior, they are projected into the future; but as objectives drawn from old, established patterns of behavior, they represent the past and they subtly place the mold of the past upon the plastic future, stamping their forms upon it. With this, the future is made unfree, and as hope is limited and inhibited in its forms, anxiety spreads its heavy aura over the psyche.

In this context, anxiety has two main aspects. As the goals of desire move forward from the past, they carry with them achievements that have already been attained; and inevitably there arises the fear that these attainments will be lost. As Lao Tse observed in the Tao Teh Ching, "To possess gives rise to the fear of losing." Correspondingly, as the goals of desire are projected into the future, there comes the fear that they will not be fulfilled. In the background of both of these fears, however, is an anxiety that comes essentially from the pressure exerted by conceptions drawn from the past in the psyche's attempt to move freely into the future. There is thus a tension of time that cramps the inner experience of the present moment, narrowing the range in which life can move and covering the individual psyche with anxiety.

Meister Eckhart, who must certainly be ranked among the greatest depth psychologists of the pre-scientific era, has understood this psychological condition profoundly and has described it within the framework of his medieval language. "Know then," Eckhart said in his Sermon No. 7 "that there is a Something in the soul in which God dwells. There is also a Something by which the soul lives in God, but when the soul is intent on external things that Something dies, and therefore God dies, as far as the soul is concerned. Of course, God himself does not die. He continues very much alive to himself."*

This "something in the soul in which God dwells" is, in its most general terms, the quality of consciousness that enables a person to recognize God in the midst of life. It is the capacity of knowing God and of responding to God in the world, the word "God" here meaning the fullness of life affirmation. But this capacity is dependent upon a particular style of consciousness for its effectiveness. When it directs itself outward, that is, in Eckhart's phrase, when it "is intent on external things," its focus becomes specific. Its range of awareness is narrowed in two ways. It is narrowed by being directed outward toward a specific point of interest which limits the area of perception and of action; and it is narrowed also because its area of perception is limited and col-

*Meister Eckhart: A Modern Translation by R. B. Blakney, p. 133.

ored in advance by the attitudes that lie behind the special desires with which it is directed outwards. It is this narrowing that closes off the soul so that it loses its capacity to be united with God. Man's relation to the infinite and unconditioned in life is cut short by his need to turn his attention to "external things."

Eckhart is here recognizing a paradox that is inherent in human existence. The potentials and aspirations that work in the depth of a person require outward expression in order for them to fulfill themselves. The imagery of the psyche requires an outer object in which it can concretize itself and in which it can be lived. Without this outer embodiment it would remain an image and an unlived potentiality that did not have the flesh and bones of life. And yet, when the psyche moves to make its vision concrete, it inevitably constricts itself and reduces the divinity that lies dormant within it. That "something by which the soul lives in God" dies when the psyche seeks to objectify itself; and yet its nature requires that it do so.

A further aspect of this problem involves the futuristic quality of the psyche. As is true of all other organs of the natural world, the psyche of the individual human being unfolds by a process of growth. It does this under the impact of its environment, primarily its social environment, which acts to draw forth the trends of development that are inherent in the psyche. This development takes place primarily by means of a movement of imagery that proceeds as a natural and continuing flow of symbols of many kinds at the nonconscious levels of the psyche.

Underlying this flow of psychic contents is a purposiveness of direction that is not conscious of itself in advance but only reveals itself as it unfolds. Its goals become visible only after the fact, after they have expressed themselves in some symbolic act or experience; but a principle of purpose underlies the whole process. The psyche moves in symbolic terms toward goals that unfold from within it. The psyche thus has nonconscious intimations of the future before it can actually embody the future and live it. This increases the tension of time that is inherent in the growth of the psyche.

The imagery that expresses the goals of the psyche comes ahead of time. It comes at each point as symbolic intimations of the next steps that are necessary for the unfoldment of the individual personaltiy. The symbol becomes the goal of the next event in life, and as it is projected out into the world so that it can be acted out and fulfilled in experience, it provides the concrete projects through which the development of the personality takes place. The affirmative feeling of life that lies behind this process of unfoldment is what we have spoken of as hope. To the degree that it carries a free and open expression, it corresponds psychologically to that "something" of which Eckhart spoke, that makes it possible for God to "dwell" within a human psyche. When hope, however, begins to become concrete and to take the form of specific desires, its quality changes.

As the imagery of the psyche provides intimations of things to come in the life of the individual, it moves the person into the future before there is anything tangible by which to measure it. This vision of the future comes with a strong energy drive behind it derived from its symbolic source, and it is experienced subjectively as possessing great strength. Nonetheless it is not yet actually present. It has announced itself, but it has not yet presented itself. A vacuum is thus created and this empty, still unfilled area is experienced as a tension of time. The goal which the psyche has spontaneously projected into the future is perceived there as a promise and as a specific hope. This means simply that it has become a desire. It is concretized in the form of desire which is then projected into the future. In the present it is felt strongly but it is not yet fulfilled. It thus leaves a vacuum in the present, and the pain of emptiness that is experienced there is greater in proportion to the intensity with which the desire has been felt.

The stronger the desire and the broader the symbolic connotations attached to it, the greater the force of the vacuum that is created. As the image of hope is projected into the future, a void is created by the emptiness of the situation in the present, and this is magnified by comparison with the promisory vision. The psychological tone that accompanies this void is anxiety. It may be rationalized in many ways. Many different reasons may be given by the individual to account for it and to explain how it has come into being; but the quality of the feeling is anxiety, heavy, brooding, fearful, tending toward panic, because the emptiness of the present does not indicate how the desire that has been projected will be fulfilled. We have here one of the psycho-dynamic forms by which hope goes into its opposite and becomes anxiety. It is the fundamental dialectic of the psyche.

9

Affirmation
and the Never Syndrome

As the *thesis*, hope, narrows itself to a specific desire, it generates anxiety, which is its *antithesis*; and the tension between them builds in the vacuum of the present moment where they meet. The urge to achieve a synthesis of these opposites and thus to relieve the inner tension increases as the pressure builds in the vacuum. This urge toward synthesis takes many forms, varying according to the temperament or "psychological type" of the individual who finds himself in such a predicament. It is instructive for us to note the main characteristics of these attempts to resolve the problem as it occurs in people who are predominantly "feeling types" or "thinking types" respectively.*

One of the main ways in which individuals attempt to resolve the impasse of anxiety is by establishing an "affirmative attitude" toward their problem. This is particularly true of persons whose temperament is characterized by a predominantly feeling tone. They seek to get a *feeling* of what is taking place within them, so that they can enter into it and gauge what is trying to work itself out in their lives. When

---

*For convenience I am following here C. G. Jung's definition of thinking types and feeling types.

they believe that they know what this is, they attempt to strengthen their image of it. They may then intensify their feeling of the goal that lies in the background of their life, and focus the full energies of the psyche to this one point. It becomes in effect a building and directing of will power to achieve the particular desires that have been important for the person.

In order to strengthen this will power and support it, there is often an attempt to build a "faith" in the eventual outcome. It must be believed in order to be successful and to come out well. Thus it is necessary to generate confidence and even enthusiasm about the final result. This increases the energy available for the project, builds the momentum, and the power of will that can be directed toward it. It increases the person's "faith" in the success he will eventually have. Often, because of the need to bolster this confidence and to draw upon a source of support that is greater than the individual's own will, this faith in achieving the hoped-for goal is placed in the context of some established religious belief. The appeal is then made to God for strength and success as the individual seeks to draw upon the ultimate and eternal power of the universe to satisfy his personal ends.

Meister Eckhart has some sharp remarks to make about this attempt to use God to achieve private desires. "Be assured," he says, in Sermon No. 19, "that when you seek your own you never find God, for you are not seeking him with purity of heart. You are seeking something along with God and you act as if you were using God, as if he were a candle with which one might look for something else and having found it, one might throw the candle away. Take it for granted that what you look for *with* God has no essential value whatever it may be, whether profit, or reward, or spirituality, or whatever. (Using God) you are looking for nothing and that is why you find nothing.*

---

*Eckhart, op. cit., p. 185.

Eckhart's conception is essentially that God the Creator is Absolute Being and that all the creaturely world is non-being. The attempt to use God to fulfill creature desires is therefore a negation of God in the special sense that it reduces being to non-being. When Eckhart says it leads to "nothing" he means that it leads to non-being. To "use" God as one uses a candle is to act toward God as though God were an object in Martin Buber's sense, and it has the effect of separating oneself from God. This is the primary psychological, and at first sight, paradoxical effect of calling upon God to fulfill the desires of the person when hope has been narrowed into desire. It separates the individual from God because it uses God as an object and because it moves increasingly from God, which is Being, in the direction of the desire, which is non-being.

Another psychological effect of calling upon God and using God to achieve a specific personal goal is that it forces the future into the mold of the past. When the image of God is symbolically conceived in the terms of an historical religious tradition, it carries the greatest concentration of energy that that culture has to offer. The individual who can feel intensely the validity of the particular symbol of God that his religious traditions provide, and who intensifies this belief by concentration and prayer, is very often able to focus sufficient energy upon a given point to achieve his desire with respect to it. When this has been done, however, God has been used as a psychological channel, as a means toward a further goal. The important question is then what the nature of that goal is. If that goal could be described as being derived from God, it would be a valid goal in Eckhart's terms; but if not, the goal would represent non-being and the whole process would involve a reduction of the image of God to the terms of non-being.

How can we determine this? By what criteria can we measure whether a goal is a valid one or not, and whether or not it is connected to God? Perhaps the best, most succinct answer is to recognize that only when a goal is not a goal is it authentic and psychologically sound.

From whence do the goals of persons come? From the psyche, which is the organ of direction and meaning in life for human beings. But the psyche, as an active organ of life is ever in flow. It is a movement of images of many kinds, visual and non-visual, that supplies the contents of consciousness. The goals of personal desire are drawn from this flow. They come forth from the movement of imagery and in their symbolic forms they project themselves, literally throw themselves forward, and establish themselves concretely as goals for future activity.

When this takes place, the style and tempo by which the psyche proceeds is radically altered. Previously it had moved forward as a self-propelling flow, carrying its own momentum, and bringing forth, out of its natural spontaneity, its new and creative achievements. Each new event came forth from it as a creative act precisely because it moved without premeditation. The power of a creative thrust was possible for it at each moment because the movement of the psyche was natural and un-self-conscious. Its products were emergents in the fullest sense of the term, new creations brought forth in freedom by the totality of the ongoing process out of which they were born.

When, however, a specific goal is projected forward as we have described it, this creative process stops. It begins with the flow of the psyche moving forward in its unpremeditated, spontaneous way, until, at some point, an image is brought forth that strikes the consciousness of the person with special impact. This is when the psyche shifts its style. The image is part of the process in the psyche by which unlived potentialities seek to bring themselves to birth. The image, appearing in a symbolic form, is one step in the sequence of inner events by which a particular potentiality will actualize itself in life. At this point in the process, the image is most probably a foreshadowing of further developments that are still latent in the depths of the psyche. It is an intimation of things to come and thus, while it is psychologically necessary for it to come forth at the very moment when it does, its appearance is also, from another point of view, ahead of time.

That the image strikes the consciousness of the individual with particuar impact is of great consequence. The conscious attempts of the individual are drawn to the image and they affirm its promise. The ego, in fact, interprets the very appearance of the image as in itself a promise. It holds to it and makes of this image an object of desire, a specific goal toward which hope is directed. This goal is a claim made against the future into which the individual projects himself. But the present is left empty, and this vacuum of time is filled with anxiety.

To counteract this anxiety in what is thought of as a constructive way, individuals often resort to deliberate concentrations of affirmative belief in seeking to bring their goal to fulfillment. What they are doing, however, is esentially an attempt to force the future to fit the mold which the present has created, and in this attempt they often use God, or more accurately their image of God, as a means toward their ends. In this, however, for reasons that we have already seen, they violate not only the nature of God but the nature of the human psyche, for their determined use of the power of the will restricts the free and open flow which the psyche requires if the full potential of time is to unfold through it.

As the promissory note which the individual holds against the future is not paid, his anxiety intensifies into panic. Increasingly it seems to him that this note he holds up to life will *never* be paid. He feels this essentially because of the split in time that opens like a chasm beneath him, fixing him in an empty present while his goal is projected into the future. His consciousness cannot bridge the gap between these two. It cannot conceive how the step will be taken from one aspect of time to another. It will *never* happen, the person feels; and this is the key to his anxiety. The word, *never*, expresses the seemingly unbridgeable void that is felt to be separating present and future.

This feeling of *never* is truly the ultimate antithesis of hope. The word itself is an indication that hope has diffused itself in desire and has brought the psyche into disorder. What began as hope has turned into hopelessness, and the person is subject then to what may be spoken of as the *Never Syndrome*. This is a point where the greatest psychological dangers arise, principally feelings of acute depression and suicide, as we saw in the case of Leo Tolstoy. The thought of suicide comes to the psyche simply as an externalization of the feeling of emptiness that is within. The thought of it passes when the void is filled, and the psyche itself is able to do this in a way that bridges the gap between the present and the future.

Seen from one point of view, the panic that grips the personality in the *Never Syndrome* arises from a misunderstanding regarding the promissory aspect of psychic imagery. The vision that comes to a person is an intimation that some new seed has taken root in the depths of the psyche and is trying to grow. It reveals itself in a dream or in another type of intuitive experience because it is in process of moving out of the psyche and projecting itself into the world. It is giving an intimation of what is trying to unfold, and it does this ahead of time, but that does not mean that the psyche is making a promise. It is indicating an intention, but it is not making a promise. There are too many contingencies in the life of the individual, and in life as a whole. When the person feels hope in the general sense in which we have described it as an affirmation of life, he does not interpret his image as a promise.

He does not have the need to believe in a promise because

he naturally trusts in life. But when hope is concretized and is projected in specific desires, it leads to expectation; and the vacuum between the present and the future draws that expectation taut. It seems then to the person that payment is not going to be made on the promissory image given by the psyche, that payment is not going to be made by God, nor by life, nor by any of the individuals with whom the person is in contact. The anxiety of *never* then sweeps over the psyche. Life itself is felt to be bankrupt. The individual writes off his existence as though it were a bad debt, and sinks into the particular style of negative psychology that fits his temperament.

10

Patience and the
Vacuum of the Present

The foregoing is a description of how persons who have primarily a feeling orientation to life experience the tension of time within themselves. It works out somewhat differently for individuals whose approach to life is primarily by thinking, *i.e.*, thinking types.

For such individuals, as the promissory images of the psyche are not fulfilled, the anxiety that results is met by intellect. They seek understanding, on the assumption that if they can achieve an intellectual perspective of their problem, they will overcome the tension of time that is within them, and they will thereby quiet their anxiety. This is an entirely reasonable conception with which to proceed, and it certainly is effective in limited situations. But it fails to answer the anxiety that arises from the tension of time in the psyche.

The attempt to develop an intellectual perspective actually increases the tension by elaborating and rationalizing it, and eventually it makes the feeling of vacuum at the center of personality more acute and more panicky. It begins with a good affirmation of the image by which the psyche gave its promise of things to come; and it then sets itself to understand sympathetically the problems that are preventing their fulfillment. It is a rational approach that seeks calm under-

standing and a perspective of time in the spirit of the
Preacher in Ecclesiastes. "For everything there is an appointed time; And there is a time for every purpose under the
heavens . . ."

This attitude of reasonableness and waiting with its tone
of mature knowing must certainly be expected to have a
calming effect upon a panicking person. That is why this is a
common style of response that is often made in friendship to
comfort a friend who is suffering from an attack of anxiety.
"Have patience," is the quieting advice thaat is frequently
given. "See things in perspective and have patience. Learn
how to wait."

Some persons do indeed learn how to wait, and they are
able to hold firm until the seed of promise in the psyche is
able to grow. But these are seldom the persons who are subject to acute anxiety. For these persons, the advice to be patient and to wait often has the opposite of a calming effect. It
seems, indeed, that for them the word *wait* frequently trig-
gers a much more intense phase of the anxiety. The very
thought of waiting makes more vivid the awareness of the
void in which the present moment is contained. To feel the
void sets the *Never Syndrome* in motion. The person is then
convinced that the emptiness of waiting will never end and
that the hoped-for desire will never be fulfilled.

In similar terms, when a person recommends to an anxious friend that he be patient with life, he is advising him to
develop an intellectual perspective of his situation. It is a sug-
gestion that he understand the problems that stand in the
way of his achieving the desires he has envisioned, and that
he give things a chance to work themselves out. This is certainly sensible counsel calculated to quiet the person's fears,
but it often has the reverse effect. Its attitude of clear thinking brings additional clarity to the subject and this places the
problem in a sharper light. The object of desire is brought
into a clearer view, both in its limitations and its futurity.

The effect is to make the person still more conscious of the abyss that is looming underneath, as happened with Tolstoy in his dream. The feeling of the void is intensified, and thus the counselling that seeks to give comfort often has the effect of increasing the panic it sought to avert. Rather than reconnect the individual with sources of life that could sustain him on a deeper than intellectual level, it cuts him off further by appealing to his reason and aggravating inadvertently the tension of time in the psyche.

What would be involved in establishing a larger connection with life capable of carrying a person over the void? It would mean that *patience* and the essence of *waiting* could be understood in an inward way, not as a disciplined biding of time until we receive full payment for our desires, but as an open attitude toward the flow of life. It would mean stepping beyond all special goals toward which desire has been directed and situating oneself in the open moment of time where life is moving freely. The definite desire makes for the tension of time, but the open attitude gives confidence in the unrestricted fullness of life, and this is hope.

Paul Tillich has understood this well. In his sermon on "Waiting," in *The Shaking of the Foundations*,* he points out that individuals who seek special objects are possessed by that which they seek to possess. Patience in such a context takes on a more active aspect. It is not merely a resigned waiting for a predetermined goal to be fulfilled. It is a participation in life in such a way that new and valid goals are able to come forth and draw themselves toward fulfillment, without being hurried but according to their own rhythm when their time is ready. The importance of a freely open attitude is that goals that are fixed in advance may artificially constrain the possibilities of development. The potentials of

---

*Tillich, Paul, *The Shaking of the Foundations*, Charles Scribner's Sons, New York, 1948, p. 149 ff.

the future are greater than a person can imagine; and they are certainly greater than can be conceived in advance by categories of thought that are derived from past experience. That is why it is important to move freely forward with an open attitude of hope.

"He who waits passionately," Tillich writes, "is already an active power himself" and this is "the greatest power of transformation in personal and historical life."*

To "wait passionately" is clearly not a passive stance. It is active involvement. It is onward movement with the flow of time, connected to life and being carried forward by the opening of each present moment of time, by the unfolding of each Now. Thus it is a great power, for the creativity that is inherent in each boundless moment of time is brought forth by the active attitude of open participation in time.

In the Western tradition of spiritual experience, a few teachers have stood forth like beacons, calling attention to a quality of life that is reached beyond time. The anonymous author of *The Cloud of Unknowing* taught the dynamic technique of breaking through "an atom of time" by a spontaneous "short prayer that pierces heaven."** And before him the greatest of them all, Meister Eckhart, sought to lead persons to experience a dimension of reality that cut through outer appearances to the core of Being.

"To say that God created the world yesterday or tomorrow would be foolishness," Eckhart wrote, "for God created the world and everything in it in the one present Now. Indeed, time that has been past for a thousand years is as present and as near to God as the time that now is."+ And again, presenting the same quality of awareness from another direction, he says, "Yesterday as I sat yonder I said something

---

*Ibid., p. 151
**See Progoff, *The Cloud of Unknowing*, A Modern Rendering with an Introductory Commentary, Julian Press, New York, 1957; Dell paperback, 1983.
+*Op. Cit.*, p. 214

that sounds incredible: 'Jerusalem is as near to my soul as this place is.' Indeed, a point a thousand miles beyond Jerusalem is as near to my soul as my body is, and though I am as sure of this as I am of being human, it is something even learned priests seldom understand. See! My soul is as young as the day it was created, yes, and much younger. I tell you, I should be ashamed if it were not younger tomorrow than it is today."*

Eckhart was not being coy or self-conscious when he said that his experience of Jerusalem sounded "incredible." The opaqueness of the material body and the definiteness of space and time are well established facts of our common-sense world. In what terms, then, can the truth of his awareness be understood? In terms of a dimension of experience that is more fundamental than sensory perception. Thus Eckhart says that time past is *as near to God* as the present is; and Jerusalem is *as near to my soul* as the place where he stands. It is the dimension of God and the soul. But this must also be understood on two levels.

On one level, God and the soul are nothing more than symbolic concepts by which a man living in Western Christendom in the middle ages could articulate and communicate his elusive inward experiences. On another level they stand for a quality of reality that lies not only beyond Christianity but equally beyond all other religious and special doctrines. It is the dimension of spiritual reality itself, and this is a dimension of life that can only be perceived in symbolic forms, although the power of the reality lies beyond the symbols and comes into the world by means of them, using them as vehicles. Upon this dimension, physical distance is overcome and the disparities of time, past, present and future, are united in a single atom of time, a Now that reaches across the fullness of being. In the awareness of this as a

*Op. Cit., p. 134

profound, intense, shaking experience of personally validated knowledge lies the answer to anxiety. To know it and to enter into it in the length and breadth, the depth and height of one's being, as the author of *The Cloud of Unknowing* says, is to move naturally and unself-consciously across the void that lies at the center of time. It is the means of reconnecting to the core of being that overcomes anxiety, that restores hope and sustains it.

11

Social Transition and Personal Feelings

The experience of *Now* which is recommended in the sermons of Meister Eckhart, in *The Cloud of Unknowing*, and more recently in the writings of Paul Tillich, represents an ultimate answer to the problem of anxiety. This is fitting inasmuch as the phenomenon of anxiety is inherent in the human condition. It is a universal problem, and therefore it would seem that to resolve it fundamentally an encounter with ultimates is required. Experience in psychotherapy during the past generation has certainly indicated that this is the case. There are, nonetheless, aspects of anxiety that are of a more transitory nature. Certain aspects of anxiety involve mainly the subjective experiences of personal life; and there are other aspects in which anxiety is a by-product of the social conflicts of history.

This leads us to two general questions that are important for our consideration both of hope and of utopia. The first is the question of whether there are psychological principles and procedures available to guide us in drawing the individual person past the subjective experience of anxiety, past the *Never Syndrome*, to a sustaining realization of time and ultimate meaning. The second is the question of the cultural factors that may be involved in the modern experience of anxiety, and whether there is any social program or attitude that can help heal the psychic breach at this point in history.

In approaching these questions it is good for us to keep in mind the close connection between social-historical factors and the individual personality. A primary function of each cultural system is that it provides a framework of beliefs and standards of behavior to serve as guidelines for individual lives. When there is conflict within the culture regarding these standards, a confusion results that tends to break old social patterns apart. The split is cultural, but it is experienced directly and intensely within the personal lives of individuals. Just as it is individuals who enact in their daily existence the values and codes of each society, so it is that in a historical period when these standards are in flux or when they are in a condition of deterioration, the pressures are felt within the individual. It is the individual who suffers then from a personal lack which may easily be interpreted in terms of pathology insofar as it results in a malfunctioning of the personality. It must be understood, however, that although it is experienced as a personal neurosis, such conditions have their source in the social transformations taking place in the background of history.

It is indeed characteristic of our time that individuals bear the psychological brunt of the cultural turmoils of the modern era. Consider, for example, the situation of a man of Algerian background living in America who came for psychological treatment. Having been brought up in Algeria under French rule, he could only perceive himself in the negative terms of a colonial subject, as a person of non-European racial background born to live in a world of Western European values dominated by persons of Western European background. He had become accustomed to view his life through the lens of a self-negating image of inferiority, and this had become the central factor in his personality leading to his several insecurities, confusions and aggressions.

Personal problems of this insecurity type are clearly a result of the intense cultural transitions that characterize the modern era. The personal forms of it are diverse because the combinations of cultures that come into conflict are varied, but the essential effect upon the individual caught in the midst of it is the same. It splinters the person by injecting feelings of inferiority and it leaves a void of anxiety at the center of the personality.

Anxieties deriving from cultural change have been common in the United States during the past two generations, especially because of the heavy mixture of populations in the American culture following World War II. The fact is, however, that the psychological tensions that accompany historical transition are common on all the continents of the world in the twentieth century. It is an indication of a major problem that the new image of Utopia is called upon to solve in our time.

In the years since the end of World War II the movement of history has been particularly turbulent and has led to many feelings of social inferiority and aggression, especially in those areas of the world that are referred to as "underdeveloped." The new programs of development designed to give these countries the characteristic stamp of the modern age are primarily technological; but the economic transformations which they bring about carry with them social and ideological changes as well. In the long run it is the latter type of change that is of the greatest importance, for it effects the individual's intimate attitudes about the conduct of personal life. Traditions of conduct that may have been entrenched for centuries can be uprooted by the new technological developments, and the changes often carry a high degree of tension and psychological disturbance for the indi-

viduals involved. We are witnessing this in areas like India
and Africa as the populations there are being drawn into the
technological advancement and personal turmoils of the
modern age.

In the United States from the very beginning of the twentieth century psychological tensions arising from the problems of social transition have been widespread. At first they
were the result of the influx of foreign groups into the country. In the decades following World War II, however, the
problems have reached far beyond the personal conflicts of
immigrant nationalities struggling to integrate themselves
into the mainstream of modern society. In the United States
as in the rest of the world the issue increasingly involves the
relative position of the major racial divisions of mankind.
The emotional problems of persons socially classified as
"negro" have led to even more pressing questions, both for
those persons who have remained at a relatively primitive
level in rural areas, and those who are seeking to participate
in the general world culture in the sciences and arts of modern civilization. But even the question of racial integration is
not primarily the Negro's problem. It shakes the emotional
heart of the white man's view of himself, of his place in the
world, and of his relation to his fellow human being. It is
experienced socially as an intense emotional conflict, and we
must become capable of seeing in it also the tensions of
growth by which a new unitary vision of mankind is struggling to come forth in the modern world. It is the molding in
the midst of history of a new utopian image.

The externals are different, but there is a similar situation
psychologically, from the point of view of the personal conflicts and confusions that are experienced, in many persons
who live by the canons of science and technology. These are
people who have been trained in scientific disciplines and are
engaged in modern technological procedures every day as

part of their vocations; but they hear another voice calling in them out of the traditions of their religious past. There is much more involved here than the voice of childhood rising again in the mature scientist. It is the whole spirit of the modern person split by the events of history and prodded by the interior need to find a believable and integrative meaning for life.

Two different cultural traditions are at work within the psyche of those modern persons whose commitment is to science and technology. They may have been brought up in Christianity or in Judaism or in any of the other religious traditions, but now they spend their working lives as scientists or as engineers or as business persons who use the products of science. They are caught in a fundamental psychological conflict with a social base that can precipitate moral dilemmas of great emotional intensity in the areas of individual conduct. The difficulties are experienced in personal life and tend to be interpreted by the individuals as involving an inferiority that is theirs alone. It is clear, however, that the problems are larger than personal. They must be seen in a larger-than-individual context as aspects of the social transitions that lead to personal confusions. Individuals often interpret the inferiority and the guilt as being their own, but by no means is it correct for them to take the whole burden of blame upon themselves. Neither should they let themselves go free of the tensions which stir in them. The more that modern persons engage themselves in these tensions, the more that they struggle in these conflicts until they are resolved, the clearer it will be that a new unitary image of life is being forged in history with them as its instruments.

A further instance of the social process working itself out through the anxieties and conflicts of individuals lies in the changing image of modern woman. From a time when the social image of woman was truly as a rib of man, dependent, protected, and living a vicarious existence through her husband-master, modern woman has emerged as a person in her own right. The modern conception of woman regards her as competent to set the terms of her own existence with an equal value to be set upon the fulfillment of her potentials as upon those of the male.

These are the two poles of social attitude, and in many women who aspire to be modern women both of these attitudes appear side by side in varying degrees. They think of themselves as modern women in the full, advanced sense of the term; and at the same time they feel impelled to live out the more dependent, earthbound image of a bygone day. The two images pull simultaneously in opposite directions, and not infrequently it seems as though they will tear the psyche apart.

Often it is just when she begins to succeed in fulfilling the new image of herself as a person that the modern woman finds herself called back to thoughts of the older style of life. Then inadvertently she begins to judge herself by the standards of the earlier social image, and by these criteria she finds herself lacking in important respects. She feels inferioir then, in the psychological sense that Alfred Adler described. But if she seeks to shift the emphasis of her life and live the riblike image of woman, the standards of the modern view rise in her and fill her with restlessness again. From whichever of the two standpoints she judges herself, she is bound to see herself as inadequate for life, with all the anxieties and aggressions to which such feelings lead.

Here again we have a situation in which the pain of anxiety is experienced personally because the individual embodies two contrary social images. It is a conflict on the level of culture and history, but the pain of it must be suffered through by individuals. On which level, then, shall the problem be resolved, the personal or the cultural? It must be both. Certainly the disequilibrium experiencd in the individual psyche must be handled with the techniques of personal psychological work. The fundamental answer, however, is to be found on the social level. A unifying ideology is required to bridge the conflicting conceptions of life that turn individual psyches into battlegrounds of history.

The very intensity of the psychological struggles that take place within modern persons is an indication that an integrative vision is indeed trying to come through. In each of the cases that we mentioned as instances of cultural conflicts being experienced as personal anxiety, a constuctive image is at work carrying a vision for the future. For example, in the African Colonial of whom we spoke, the feeling of belonging to an inferior group was more than balanced by his intuition of the fact that he would discover his identity not as an African but as a human being. The image working in him was that of a person who would eventually be able to participate in a world civilization, the civilization of the modern arts and sciences, in which all human beings could have an opportunity to develop their talents and find their place regardless of their origins or their social circumstances.

We must certainly understand this as a vision of utopian quality. It carried a social image psychologically projected into the future by the individual, comparable to the process by which the psyche projects its images of hope. As a utopian image, a social expression of hope, it came ahead of time and thus it left a vacuum that was filled by anxiety according to the pattern followed by the dynamics of hope, as we have seen. That vision was ahead of its time of fulfillment, not only for the Algerian man to whom it came, but it was ahead of time also for our society as a whole. The fact that it came to him, however, as its equivalent comes to others indicates that it is actively working to fulfill itself, albeit in the background of events. This is an aspect of the image of utopia that is a social dream unfolding through the behavior of individuals in the modern world.

Not different from the Algerian, the scientist of whom we spoke who finds himself torn by allegiance to the tradition of an inherited religion as well as to the traditions of science also has an unfulfilled vision behind his personal experience. While two historical views of truth struggle within him, he has an intimation of a truth that transcends the two and draws them together in a single vision. This image also is ahead of time, but it is the utopian image of a new unitary truth to come that motivates many to work in the sciences while hoping for a spiritual vision as well.

Similar to the colonial man and the scientist in the image of hope that lies behind her negations, is the modern woman whom we mentioned, the woman who is torn between the old image of dependent femininity and the feeling that the seed of a whole person is growing in her. Beyond her self-condemnations, guilts, and anxieties, lies the intuitive knowledge that she will eventually establish her identity free of the historical stereotypes of woman so that her existence will express a newly emerging image of what woman can become as a human being in a new age.

In each of these representative situations the anxiety is balanced by an image of larger potential in the person's existence. This is an image of what is possible in the future, and its effect is indeed to stretch the tension of time that leads to the anxiety. In each case the image is not merely personal, but is inherently social. Each has a utopian quality, whether as a unitary vision of overcoming the separateness of man among the nations, as intimations of a unitary truth connecting the sciences and religion, or as a vision of a fuller unfoldment of life for women. Each is reaching toward a larger than personal perspective in which anxiety can be overcome by meaning. This is the constructive quality of the utopian image as a psychological factor. It reaches out of anxiety with an image of the future that is social as well as personal, and it therefore has a connective and healing effect.

Such images appear in many individuals who possess in greater or less degree the qualities of the utopian person. The images they bring forth are meaningful not only for themselves but for the community as a whole because they all contribute to the large unitary view of life that is needed as a new frame of reference for the modern world. The more utopian imagery that individuals stir in themselves, the sooner will the new unitary vision become an actuality in the modern experience of life.

The question we must put to ourselves, therefore, is by what means can an image of utopia be evoked in modern times so that it will bring a vision large enough to meet the needs of our civilization? The answer to this involves a psychological principle and process, the essence of which is expressed in the lives of the utopian persons of the past. We saw an instance of it in Leo Tolstoy, in the tremendous inward suffering through which he lived and in the way this suffering finally stirred a deep and dark image in him out of which a new vision of life was formed. This was a social vision. It related to the community of mankind as a whole; but its source was the psyche of an individual. By the tensions of personal conflict, it had been drawn from the transpersonal depths of the psyche. We saw there that, though the utopian image had a special meaning for the individual in whom it was formed, it also possessed much more than individual significance.

We may well regard this process in a utopian person like Tolstoy as a prototype of the social process by which modern man will discover the new image of utopia that is needed. The difference is that, in order to form a new image that will meet the need of our times, the experience of it must come not merely to a single utopian individual but to many persons in the modern community. It must happen to many that they are drawn into the depths of the psyche by tensions and confusions that shake the personal psyche with anxiety until an image of transpersonal meaning is brought forth to give a new context to life. Cumulatively, as such experiences happen to many persons in the modern world, a distinctive tone and quality of perception will enter the community. The utopian vision that will reshape our times will then not involve a doctrine to be believed in as a faith, nor as an intellecutally conceived philosophy. It will come forth rather out of the consensus and cumulative tone of many individual experiences taking place on the symbolic level of the psyche and formed by images that reflect deeper-than-conscious intimations of truth.

These experiences may occur with great force and power in certain highly sensitive psyches, especially in the creative type we have called the utopian person. Beyond these, however, if it is to reach into the tissue of our times, it must be brought forth out of the flow of life itself. The new image of utopia which our time requires will be produced not by the great leadership personalities, but by the cumulative experiences of Everyman and Everywoman suffering through the conflicts of modern times and drawing out of the anxieties of the psyche new visions of life.

In this perspective we should speak not of *an* image of utopia, but of the *imagery* of utopia. It is a flow of imagery that is involved, a movement of many images coming from the psychic depths of many persons and reflecting the inner stirring and the great longing of modern human beings. Not one image of utopia, not a blueprint, nor a program, nor a specific ideal, but a large movement of images carrying an intimation of a new context in which the impasses of modern society will be resolved. As the colonial inferiority feeling of the Algerian man carried with it an image of the equality of mankind; and as the religious and moral conflicts of the scientist carry with them an image of the ultimate integration of scientific investigation and man's spiritual quest; so also, modern woman's confusion as to the role and possibilities of her life carries an image of the full and free development of persons.

In all these instances the dialectical quality of the psyche is at work. A disturbance in each case draws forth an image that opens the way to a new and constructive possibility. Each image speaks for the future, setting forth a condition that is brought forth ahead of time, before its fulfillment is possible. Thus it involves hope, though the hope may not be consciously articulated. And the social expression of hope is an image of utopia, a fore-visioning of life as it may be possible for human beings to live it together.

Out of the depths of many modern persons' psyches, there comes the imagery that expressed the social hope of our time. This is the imagery of utopia forming itself, giving itself body and content, establishing the possibilities of the future while it is still in the midst of the struggles of the present.

12

Twilight Imaging and Utopian Persons

We come to the question at this point of whether there are methods by which we can assist in forming a new utopian vision for modern times. We understand that while a utopian vision involves social hope, it can come only through the experience of individuals and in the lives of individuals. It is a personal work that may have a social outcome.

In general there are two ways of approach for the individual. One is to move with the pressures of the anxiety in the midst of one's life, feeling the impact of events and exploring their implications as they happen. Taking this path, we let the inner conflict intensify itself within us, increasing the struggle between the polarities in our psyche. But we are aware of what is happening, even as we let it happen. This is important. Strange dreams and other imagery experiences are then bound to arise, often in an atmosphere of inner unpleasantness. We saw these in the life of Leo Tolstoy. Eventually, if we stay with the disturbances and suffer through the whole process, the deepening of the symbolic level leads to a resolution; or it leads at least to a fuller, more deeply-based awareness of the conditions and meaning of human existence. There are, we discover, experiences and understandings that are of greater value than merely resolving our personal problems, much as we may wish to do that.

There is a deepening movement within us and an accompanying awareness that reach beyond the healing of our personal pains. It draws our consciousness into contact with the ultimates of human existence. We saw this also in the life of Tolstoy. A portion of harmony came in the midst of great pain; and considerable disharmony remained in his life. Having struggled through the polarities that raised difficult questions both for his personal life and for his life as a human being, Tolstoy came by means of his anxiety dream to an integrating awareness. The dream gave him a symbol of elemental strength as well as a personal contact with a larger dimension of reality. His individuality then had a context. Having continued with unsureness through the cycles of the process, Tolstoy received the connection to life that enabled him to pass across the void of anxiety that had formed within him. His experience on the symbolic level gave him an image of utopian quality, an image with the capacity to heal both himself and other human beings living in his time. Of the greatest importance, it gave him an image with which he could eventually relate to the continuing movement of opposites in human existence. Tolstoy's experience is an instance of how one can work inwardly in the midst of personal life toward an integrative awareness that is larger than personal. It is the way of the intensification of the inner conflict, and it involves the principle of symbolic unfoldment.

The second way that can be followed is a much quieter and more relaxed approach. Rather than intensify the conflict, the individual lets go of his specific problem. He gives it up, at least for the moment, letting it float freely on the surface while he goes down into the depths. For this deliberate descent into the psyche, a specific method that has been developed in the practice of depth psychology is suggested.

The method of *Twilight Imaging* is a procedure whereby
the individual lets go of the contents of his waking consciousness, relaxes, closes his eyes, possibly lying down while
he does so if this relaxes him better, and permits himself to
see, feel, hear, or sense in a generalized way images that
come upon the inner screen of the mind. These images may
be visual; they may be auditory, olfactory, verbal, or they
may carry intuitive perceptions of the possibilities of the future as intimations are given to the person at the nonconscious level. Whatever sensory form they take, and they
may be experienced in all these forms, it is most important
for the purposes of Twilight Imagery that the individual not
attempt to influence the style of the images. The flow must
be totally free, and the person must hold himself in the position of being an altogether neutral observer. He must permit
himself to *behold* his imagery, and never to create it with
deliberate purpose.

Whichever method is followed, whether the intensification of the inner conflict or the more relaxed way of evoking
the psyche by *Twilight Imaging*, the ultimate result is that a
large, integrative and connective symbol is brought forth
from the depth of the psyche. In either case, the key lies in
the continuity of the movement of symbolic material. If the
dream process is worked with consecutively, it will eventually bring forth from the midst of the anxiety the deeper,
encompassing image that carries the new vision. Similarly, if
the *Twilight Imaging* procedure is followed regularly, there
will eventually emerge out of its natural unfoldment an image that carries a transpersonal perspective for the person's
life. This is one of the results that emerge from the process of
symbolic unfoldment.

We should note that these two ways are not mutually
exclusive. They complement each other so that it can be helpful to combine them. Used together, they can build a rhythm
of alternating tension and relaxation into the process of evok-

ing the depth images of the psyche. The material that comes from the depth of the psyche has, however, an ambiguous aspect. On the one hand it contains the guidance of the inner wisdom. On the other hand it comes in the form of symbols that do not make clear their meaning for the individual's life. There is thus a gap between the symbolic experiences and a person's perception of the several levels of messages that are carried by these symbols, whether they are dreams, twilight images, or the events of life. One of the functions of the *Intensive Journal* process has been to fill this gap, to provide a vehicle by which, in the context of a person's life as a whole, the several levels of messages that come from the depth can be explored. Thinking of the life of a person like Tolstoy, it is possible that his integrative experiences could have taken place sooner, less painfully and with richer stimulations for his creativity if he had had such an instrument available to him.

One of the great insights of C. G. Jung concerned the nature of fairy tales. He recognized them to be the folk dreams of the earlier generations of mankind, symbolic stories drawn from the deeper-than-personal levels of the psyche. In modern times the equivalent of fairy tales may also appear in the dreams of individuals or, with even greater facility, in twilight imaging experiences. The experience that is told in the following pages is such a fairy tale that came to a woman of middle years, Mrs. F., as a series of images in the twilight state. As the process of Twilight Imaging continued, its symbolism deepened beyond the personal, enabling us to see what is involved in being a Utopian Person in the modern world.

"The king wore a golden crown, an ermine robe, and a pleased expression on his face. 'Bring forth the royal treasure chest', he ordered his attendant.

"Seated next to the king upon a throne as large as her father's was the Princess Marcia, sitting straight and sad as she twirled a large ring upon her small finger. The ring contained the largest ruby in the kingdom.

"Obeying the king, the attendant placed the treasure chest upon a low table in front of them. A gold crown encrusted on the lid of the chest gleamed with emeralds. When the heavy lid was lifted, three trays of dazzling jewels became visible. In the first tray were the sapphires and the diamonds, under that the rubies and the emeralds, and in the bottom tray were glowing pearls.

"'Marcia', the king exulted, 'choose, my dear—which shall it be this year? What gem will you have for your thirteenth birthday? Nothing is too good for my little princess.'

"Marcia's thin lips were pressed together. Suddenly a gleam came into her large eyes brighter than the flash of the diamonds. She put forth her tiny foot and kicked the royal jewel chest off the table. The jewels scattered in a dazzling shower over the throne room floor.

"After a suspended moment of amazement, the page scrambled after the jewels and replaced them in the royal treasure chest. The Princess Marcia hastily left the throne room.

"That evening the king consulted his wisest counselors as to his daughter's behavior. They pulled their beards and whispered together. Finally they said, 'Oh King, is there anything the Princess Marcia has ever asked for?'

"'She has everything she wants', the king replied, 'everything she ever asked for, except of course the horse—which I could not give her because of the danger to her life. She must live to be queen when I die.'

"After more beard pulling and more whispering, the counselors bowed low before the king.

"'Oh King, we advise you to give the Princess Marcia a horse.'

"The king protested. 'But a horse will take her away from me. She will ride forth and will not sit at my side. She does not want to become queen, and a horse will make her less interested than ever in the affairs of state. It will take her away from her studies.'

"Nevertheless, a dainty black mare with a long, black mane and tail was selected for the princess, and she rode forth to her heart's content, through the high grass, across pebbly brooks, and into the cool woods. She spent less and less time with her father and her studies of state affairs, but she wore a happy look on her face.

"One day, quite far from the castle, her mare cast a shoe, and the Princess Marcia stopped at a cottage to ask for help. She was surprised to see how bare the cottage was, how ragged the children in it, and how bent over and sad the mother.

"Not knowing this was the princess, the mother said, 'Rest yourself, pretty lady, and my man will see to your mare. I have some tea, bless you, and I'll put the pot on. I have nary a crust to offer you, as the children are hungry and the taxes must be paid. If the king only knew, if he only knew how hard we struggle, and he sits there in his golden crown and his ermine robe.'

"That night the king saw that the Princess Marcia's lamp was still glowing late into the night. He found her seated at a large table, studying state affairs.

"'It is rather late, my dear', he ventured.

"'Oh, I know, Father, but I must study and learn because I am going to be queen some day.' She sat very straight in her chair and smiled."

It became clear as soon as the fairy tale was told that it was full of personal significance for Mrs. F. It recapitulated the general outlines of her earlier life and it indicated both with a disarming *naiveté* and a keen insight the trend of development that was to follow.

She had been the daughter of a very wealthy man, one who had founded a major American company and who ruled very much like a king in his own domain. As her father's youngest, she had been sheltered from the outside world, given everything that she could imagine to ask for including a fine education; but she was discouraged from any serious activities outside her father's realm. She idolized her father, but the image aptly reveals the resentment that lay within her. Her revolt came when she kicked over the treasure chest and said, "No" to her father's wishes. She had done this in her own life, albeit rather timidly.

When Mrs. F. had graduated from college, she had wanted to undertake a professional career; but her father forbade it as unbecoming for a girl in her station of life. She bowed to her father's wish that she not venture independently into the world, but she rebelled to the extent that she used marriage as an occasion for escaping from family control. This was akin to her riding the horse out into the world. The equivalent of the horse's having an accident and casting its shoe was the troubles that she encountered in her marriage. The marriage broke up, and when it did, she was thrown out into the midst of the world where she had an opportunity to achieve a much larger knowledge of other people's experience in life. With this she gained a fuller incentive and perspective for study and work in the world, and she devoted herself to these activities with the same joy as the princess in the fairy tale studying late into the night.

The fairy tale gave a concise recapitulation of past events leading up to the present moment. The present was the midst of the fairy tale, in the same sense as in a dream in which the past and future intersect. The future may be indicated in a dream, as in the fairy tale, in the form of a previsioning of later stages in the development of the psyche. Thus the fairy tale dramatized the essence of the problems of Mrs. F.'s past and gave her a promise of full and free participation in life that would become possible for her. After this previsioning on the dream level, it is still necessary to continue the symbolic process of the deep psyche in order to bring the process to fulfillment.

One of the main procedures that we used to draw the movement of the psyche along was the method of *Twilight Imaging*. This left the immediate problems of life to float on the surface while we encouraged the flow of symbolic contents at the depth of the psyche. The best way in which to communicate the elusive nature of this psychic flow is to describe the actual contents of a session of *Twilight Imaging*. One should keep in mind that what is important is not the analytical interpretation of the symbolic material, regardless of the interpretive theory that is followed, but the stimulation of the flow of the imagery. In the course of its active movement, the imagery gives us the information and the energy with which to carry out its purposes. It provides the material with which the stalemates of life can be overcome. The report of the following sessions is based on the transcript of the sessions themselves. They are of interest both as examples of the movement of imagery in the psyche and as a spontaneous expression of the depth image of Utopia emerging in a modern person.

Mrs. F.'s session began with an image of brightly lighted water that formed a stream that moved upward with considerable force and speed. That stream moved upward into the sky, and as it did so it arched itself so that it had the shape of a rainbow. As it curved in the sky, however, the stream of water reflected the light of the sun and this made it very bright and beautiful.

Being within the image, seeing it and participating in it with her eyes closed, Mrs. F. reported her feelings to me while in the midst of the experience. "The water seems to come from within me," she said. "It seems to flow out of me, and at the same time I am in it. The main thing is that it has great power and great light, and it flows in one direction. It is like a rainbow going miles up in the air. I am way up in the sky suspended by this water. There are no stairs to walk down; and there is no tower that high to stand on. So being up there, I just have to walk on the water.

"I am walking along very carefully. I am afraid to look down for fear that I will fall. I don't look down, but I see the water out of the corner of my eyes. I see the sides of the water and I feel sure that if I follow them as guidelines, I won't fall off. I just keep walking along very carefully, and now it doesn't seem so dangerous to me. I am beginning to enjoy it, and especially I enjoy the warmth of the sun. I am walking on the water but I feel that I can also lie in it and rest in it and that I will be supported by it.

"Now it seems to be gradually curving back down to the ground. I am back on the earth now, on a hard piece of rock. There is no grass around me. Just a sloping piece of rock, wet from the water and very slippery. Now I am at a sharp and jagged edge. If I fall I would go down about a thousand feet. It is very hard walking because it is so slippery and there is such a steep slope. And there is such a great abyss on the side. I see some trees ahead, but they seem to be a great distance off. It is getting darker now and I don't know if I can reach the trees. I have a very strong feeling that I don't want to be near that edge when it gets dark, so now I am walking as fast as I can.

"It has gotten quite dark, but I have just reached the trees. It feels cool and nice. In the darkness I can't tell which way to go, but I feel safer with the trees. I am groping around with my hands and I feel my way to a kind of rock-covered ledge that gives protection from the rain. It must be a cave of some sort, but in the darkness I can't tell. There could be wild animals in it, but I don't have much choice. I go in and I rest there."

After a pause Mrs. F. continued. "Now it seems to be getting light again and I find myself on a white road. It is all made of marble, and as I go along it I come to a city of marble. I am very close to the city now, about ten feet away from it. The road is very smooth and very easy to walk on; and it goes straight to the center of the city. It is like a village piazza, and there is a circle there with a statue in the center and people sitting around on benches enjoying the sun. They are very friendly.

"I find myself talking to a woman there and I am telling her about the water and all that has just happened to me. But she doesn't seem to know what I am talking about. She tells me that right here they have everything that they want, so they never have a desire to go to any other place. She wants me to stay here, but I tell her that I will just visit here for a week or two and after that I will go on."

At this point our session came to a close. At the next session I followed my usual procedure of re-establishing the atmosphere of the imagery in a hypnogogic manner, and then reading back to Mrs. F. a transcript of the previous session's twilight-imaging experience. In this way she was brought back into the context of her deep psyche and its symbolism could continue to unfold.

We went back into the imagery situation to the point where Mrs. F. was speaking with the woman in the white marble city. There was a considerable pause during which Mrs. F. seemed to be intensely engaged in some inward activity. Finally she spoke and said to me, still with her eyes closed and looking inward, "Yes, she was right. Everything was very peaceful there and it seemed right to stay. So I stayed longer. There were no clocks and no calendars, so I lost track of time. And I thought of all the dangers of walking out in the sky, being on the precipice, and how uncomfortable it was staying out all night in the cave. And I realized in comparison how safe I was here, how entirely safe, and I knew then why people didn't leave, just as the woman had said.

"But I had the feeling that these people were just sitting around; and I didn't see how they could be completely content to just sit there in the sun under the trees and do so very little work. There was a kind of dullness about the people, and I felt that I was getting duller and duller. That's why I felt that I had to leave.

"Now I have gone out on the road, and I find that the air is very exhilarating. It is so sharp and clear, and I can see the clear color of the mountains. I feel exceptionally wide awake and alive and as clear as the air. I don't know what will happen, but I feel that it is better than being with the people in the city. It was stultifying to stay with them.

"Now I seem to realize that no one else left the marble city. There was a path by which one could leave, which was the path that I had taken; and apparently some people had used that road in the past and had left. But it seemed that the people in the city didn't like it to be known that this had happened, and so they kept it a secret.

"All around me now there is snow, and also greenery. And out at the horizon there is a yellow glow of light. I think that I will stay here because this must be just as near as I can get to the stars. I think I'll stay here all through the night.

"It gets dark now, and I can see all the sky there is because there are no higher mountains. The sky is just filled with stars, just crammed with them. They seem a great silver bowl over my head. They are so bright, and the moon is so bright, that I think I could walk down the other side of the mountain by their light. So I do that. I walk down by moonlight, and it is no different than if I had done it by daylight.

"Everything seems so soft and gentle by moonlight. I realize now that there is something different about me, and it is because I have come down the mountain by moonlight. I have a different quality in me than I had before. I feel a sort of softness in me. Things don't seem so sharp, perhaps because they are bathed in the moonlight. And I seem to be the same color as the snowy path that I am walking on.

"Now I come back down to a place where there are trees, and where there isn't any more snow. I come to a tree that has very low branches, and I have the feeling that I can make my bed in it. I do that, and I am lying there now suspended in my bed in the branches of the tree. And there is nothing in the world now but the moon and myself. I am just suspended there, floating, as the moon is.

"And now I feel that the moon is speaking to me. It is as though she is a woman speaking. She tells me that she has been trying to get me to leave the city for a long time. I ask her why she hasn't talked to me before and why she hasn't told it to me as she is telling me now. She says that if she had spoken before I would not have heard her voice. But apparently I am able to hear her now because I am in the tree.

"I ask her what is to become of me now that I am in the tree. She says to me, "Well, now you can see how large the world is. There are many things that can happen to you. Life isn't as cramped and as narrow here as it is in the city. It is really wide open."

"I ask her where she will guide me. I tell her that I want her to guide me. She answers that she shines every night and that when she does she illuminates all things, and that can guide me. But she says that I myself have to choose.

"I tell her that I wish I could be this tree and just stay here forever. But she answers that the fact is that I am not this tree. She says, 'You have to be what you are'. I know that she is right.

"So I rest a while, and now I am getting ready to leave. I go down the hill and it is getting warm so I take off my heavy coat and leave it. The path is quite stony now and still very narrow. Rocks stick out on both sides so that I can hardly get through. I am becoming unsure of myself now, and I wonder if this path ever has an end. I wonder if I just have to go on this way forever. But now I seem to be coming to a clearing in the woods.

"There is a spring here and there is a cup beside it. I can drink from the spring and I do. It is fresh water. I thought I was alone, but suddenly there are about fifteen people there beside me. They are making a great fuss over me. They are so glad that I have come here. They say that they have been watching me and that they have been hoping I would get here.

"I tell them that I don't know where I am. They say to me, 'Don't you see, you are at the spring and you can drink the water'.

"I drink more of it and I find that drinking this water does give me a very different kind of feeling. It makes me feel much more optimistic. It makes me feel much happier. And all these people seem to be very happy. And now they tell me that they are all people who have left the city. They say that from where they are at the spring they can see right into the city, and that they have been watching me. They watched me when I was in the marble city and they were hoping I would leave. They say that they have been watching me as I have been coming down the road. They saw all my troubles and all my dangers, and they have been hoping I would make it. Now they are very glad that I have come. I feel very comfortable with these people. They seem to like me.

"I really still don't know where I am going, but I feel that I have arrived at some place important now. This seems to be a good stopping point. Well, not really a stopping point; more a starting point. I think they will go on further with me, and I ask them if they will. They have all gone on, they say, and now they are telling me that they have all visited many different places, but that they always come back to the spring.

"They tell me that they like to welcome people who come to the spring because these are the people who have left the city. They tell me that the way it is is that when you leave the city you have to do it by yourself. And when you arrive at the spring, you stay a while, but then you leave it also by yourself. That is what they all have done. But then when you leave it, you always come back. You come back to refresh yourself at the spring, and then you leave it again.

"I feel that I understand what they are telling me. Being at the spring feels like a home. I know that I can leave it at any time, and I know that I will leave it, and that I will return whenever I want to. It seems to be very good for me to be here now."

There are several points of view from which a sustained imagery experience of this scope can be interpreted. Certainly it has a subjective aspect that reflects the past experiences of the individual's personal life. It expresses the person's life history in symbolic form and this gives many "leads" for private work by means of the Journal Feedback method.

The second point of view from which the imagery can be understood is as an expression of the growth of personality as larger capacities of awareness emerge by means of the process of symbolic unfoldment. Through the movement of the imagery a greater depth of personality is touched and a new perspective for life takes shape. In this aspect the psyche uses its past experiences as a platform for a leap into the future.

The third aspect of the imagery is as a personal religious experience, a point of symbolic contact that opens access to larger dimensions of reality. In this aspect the individual gains increased strength for living and does so through an experience that is specifically spiritual in style even though it tends not to use traditional religious symbols.

In its fourth aspect the imagery experience must be regarded in its more than personal significance. The momentum of the imagery not only carries forward the psyche of the individual to a further stage of awareness, but it represents a further development of the psyche of the times, of the *Zeitgeist* in a very special sense, as well. This point is of particular importance because of its implications for the image of Utopia in the modern world. Deep transpersonal experiences of the psyche not only heal the individual person to whom they come, but they bring a measure of healing to the community of man as a whole. We have to consider this in greater detail, but first let us look more closely at each of the four aspects of the imagery experience.

As an expression of her personal experiences, the imagery depicts the difficult journey of Mrs. F's life. There is brightness in it, but there are times when it is a precarious journey along the edge of a precipice. The city of marble very probably corresponds to the prosperous suburban world in which Mrs. F. spent most of her life, especially the years of her marriage. It presented an atmosphere of contentment and self-contained complacency. The people there felt no need to go anywhere else, believing they already possessed everything they could possibly desire. Life was safe and comfortable there, and so they closed their eyes to all their limitations. Although people do leave the white marble city in search of a more meaningful life, those who remain keep up the pretext that no one ever leaves. In that way they avoid having to face any basic questions about themselves, and their complacency is never shaken. But as Mrs. F. said, "I felt that I was getting duller and duller. That's why I felt that I had to leave." This was the essence of the inner conflict she had felt in her life at the point where a basic change seemed to be needed. She had to find the road that would take her to a more open atmosphere in which she would find not only a larger freedom but, of even greater importance, an environment in which to explore her ultimate concerns about life.

The psychological situation in which Mrs. F. was living was represented in her imagery. By discussing its symbolism we could see the circumstances of her life and the conflict that had built within her over the years. But that is the static representational aspect of the symbolism of the psyche. In their veiled forms, the symbols describe the inner condition of the psyche; and their symbolic descriptions can be deciphered and understood. The insights from this, however, refer to the situation in the psyche at a given moment of time, like a "still" photograph taken from the continuity of a motion picture film. In order for analysis to take place, the ongoingness of the process of the psyche must be stopped; and to that degree the condition in the psyche is falsified by the very fact of analysis.

The essence of the psyche is movement. It is movement, whether forward movement expressed as development and growth, or reverse movement, which is retrogression and eventual breakdown. Because this is the fact, those symbolic expressions of the psyche that take the form of movement are much truer representations of what is taking place in the depth of the human being. Thus the imagery experience of

Mrs. F. depicts the psychological situation in which she was living—a situation that can be understood analytically if we hold the flow of the imagery as a "still" for an instant—but it also represents the motion with which her psyche was actively moving out of the conditions of her past in the direction of a new context for her life. This continuity of development, reflected in the flow of the imagery, is of the greatest importance because it is true to the dynamic, active, inward quality of human existence.

The fact of motion, which is the essence of the psyche, is represented in the imagery by the repeated journeys on which Mrs. F. has to embark. The symbol of the journey is of course an apt representation of the movement quality of the psyche, and thus it appears throughout the historical literature of spiritual growth in many variations, as the pilgrimage, the quest, the "pilgrim's progress", and so on. Here it takes the form of the road through the mountains and of a dangerous trip along a ridge with a deep abyss below; and it appears again as the image of repeated departures and returns, leaving the stream and coming back to it as a source of strength.

The journey and the necessity of being repeatedly on the road is indicative of the restless process of growth at work in Mrs. F's life. The psyche is in motion within her, and the imagery that expresses this motion at the depth level of the psyche depicts the style of the motion as well as the tone of the movement taking place. In a general sense this movement involved for Mrs. F. the unfolding of latent potentials of experience becoming real in her life in the midst of anxiety and confusion. In the imagery, the anxiety was expressed by the narrow road through the mountains and the precarious walk along the edge of a dangerous chasm. The confusion was shown in the uncertainty of the journey, not knowing where to go, not being sure at first whether to remain in the marble city or when to leave it; and not knowing what the next destination was to be nor how she would get there. Anxiety and confusion characterized the journey, but it proceeded none the less; and by its own momentum it reached a goal that could not have been anticipated. In specific personal terms, the journey represented a critical point of transition through which Mrs. F. was then passing, the transition from living in the structured environment of her suburban social situation, her marble city, to the large perspective of a free spiritual existence. The imagery expressed this passage, which was then in process of taking place.

This transition from one life situation to another involved a marked tension of time of the type of which we have spoken. This tension stirred elements within her at a level much deeper than that of subjective mental contents. It aroused images of a more than personal nature. These, being present in the depths of the psyche in a dormant form, were brought to life by the tension between the future and the past, and they were carried forward by the flow of symbols stimulated by the practice of Twilight Imaging. The dangerous passage through the mountains as part of the necessity of leaving the marble city was such a symbol. So also was the feeling of exhilaration that went with the crisp air of the mountains, and also the feeling of a new personal softness associated with the quality of the moonlight. Here the time of transition was felt most intensely, and it was a moment in limbo. Thus she was suspended in the branches of the tree, not rooted anywhere, but for the moment floating in life. Into this void there came a symbolic experience of the greatest significance. The conversation with the lady of the moon was a dialogue with a guiding principle of inward knowing, and from it she acquired a sense of direction. After this, she was no longer adrift in life. Now Mrs. F. had a point of contact with a source of knowledge greater than her own personal understanding. Once she had opened this conversation she could have access to the image of the Lady of the Moon again and again by means of this same style of symbolic dialogue, and through it she would have a source of guidance for moments of confusion that might lie ahead.

In the imagery, this guidance enabled Mrs. F. to find her way to the spring, even though she had not known in advance that it was this she was seeking. The spring provided a further point of contact for her. When she drank from it, she felt strongly reassured as to the validity of her journey. She recognized from it, and from the fifteen people at the spring, that now she had come to a place at which the powers of life could ever be renewed. She understood that she could leave the spring and always return to it from wherever she had gone. She had come actually to a place that was beyond time and space and to which therefore she would always have access. In a later session of Twilight Imagery this realization deepened still further for Mrs. F. as she recognized that the spring with its powers of renewal was accessible to her wherever she would be. Once having been there, she realized, she would not have to return to the same place again and again. Wherever she would be, the power of the spring would be accessible to her upon a dimension of experience not limited by space and time.

In this aspect of her imagery, Mrs. F. had made contact with a symbolic principle that could restore power to her personal existence. The symbols involved, and the dimension of reality that they represent must certainly be understood to be more fundamental than the personal and subjective aspects of Mrs. F.'s life experience; but just because of this, they opened a new major power in her psyche and made this power available to her as a source of strength and awareness in her personal existence. This encounter with elemental symbols of a transpersonal quality meant for Mrs. F., as it does for any person to whom it occurs, that both her mental attitude and her life could change because a new context of meaning had been given to her. The question of whether it had been given to her from within herself or from beyond herself is beside the point, for that would only be to spacialize an inherently nonspacial aspect of human experience. What is important is that the symbolic experience provided for her a point of contact with a more than personal dimension of reality through which her individual capacities for living could be enlarged.

An experience of this type becomes a resource for the personality, but it has consequences that reach beyond the individual as well. This is the fourth aspect of the imagery experience. Symbols of this type are not the sole property of the individual to whom they come. They do not belong to the person alone but rather to the collectivity of the community in which he or she lives. In primitive communities this is well known, and it has been frequently pointed out by modern anthropologists. When an individual in a primitive tribe has a dream or vision that has implications beyond his personal existence, he does not hold it for himself, but he shares it with others in the tribe who decide what is to be done with it. A good dramatic and readable instance of this is Laurens van der Post's semi-fictional novella, *Flamingo Feather*.

A significant step past primitive culture in this respect was the experience of the Biblical Prophets. Their visions were also felt to be of more than personal meaning, and thus they also were shared with the community as a whole. To judge from the Biblical texts, there was a period in the history of Israel when the public sharing of visionary experiences was an accepted event considered to be not at all out of the ordinary. Some of these symbolic encounters had an especially strong impact upon the community and were remembered and referred to for generations after they were first told. Some of these visions would become part of the oral traditions of the people handed down from century to century. And of these, a few, like the visions of Isaiah and Ezekiel, were permanently inscribed as belonging to the sacred history of the people.

In modern Western civilization we do not have a comparable attitude toward such experiences and thus we have no culturally approved way to integrate them into the ongoing life of the community. Occasionally in recent centuries a particularly intense or dramatic visionary experience has led to the founding of a new religion or cult. The establishment of the Swedenborgian Church on the basis of the visions of Emanuel Swedenborg, or the founding of the Mormon Church on the basis of the experiences of Joseph Smith are instances of this. Aspects of it are found also in the lives of George Fox, John Wesley and Martin Luther. Mainly, however, and especially in the most recent generations, modern Western civilization is not attuned to the dimension of reality that lies behind symbolic experiences, and it has no means of making what is valid in them accessible to the life of the community. None the less, it is precisely from this source that a new vitality can be secured for the spiritual life of our time. Symbolic encounters that take place upon the imagery level of the psyche have the dual quality of strengthening the personal lives of the individuals to whom they come, and of contributing larger spiritual vision to the community as a whole. In this sense, visionary experiences of the type evoked in the psychological work with Mrs. F. must be understood as increments to the deep psychological and spiritual resources with which modern Western man can face the problems of our time.

We would not classify a person like Mrs. F. as a Utopian Person, and yet the style and quality of her experience meet many of the criteria of a Utopian Person that we mentioned earlier. We would not classify her in this category for the largely superficial reason that Mrs. F. is not a person of the power or the stature of a Tolstoy or a Gandhi or a Schweitzer. She is not a person of sufficient strength to remake a segment of society in the terms of her own vision. And yet her life experience as a whole does display the main traits of the Utopian Person. She too suffered through a period of acute anxiety and brought forth out of her intense personal need a unitary vision of reality. And for her, also, the vision was meaningful not only as a means of personal healing but as a transpersonal connection to her fellowman.

We should certainly not overlook the significance of the fact that it was not a great historical figure but a modest modern woman to whom this Utopian-type image came. It is an important clue to the image of utopia that is called for in our time, for it indicates that the image of utopia which our time requires is primarily to be formed out of the experience of individuals. It is not to come into being as fulfilling the prototype of a community conceived in terms of some doctrine; for that, by extraverting the vision, only falsifies it. Further, if the image of utopia is hardened into a doctrine, it must lose the life-giving quality that can be its main contribution to an evolving society. It would then become a projection of hope which, having been thrust forward into the future leaves a vacuum in the present, a vacuum that is inevitably filled by anxiety.

We have seen in earlier pages some of the psychological aspects of how hope becomes anxiety in the lives of individuals. It is familiar to us also on the social level in the history of Utopians where doctrinal hopes have left only disillusionment. Social programs tend to fall into the same cyclical patterns that are the result of the dialectical principles in individual human lives. Social programs are, after all, the products of individual human beings. They express the individual's experience of imagination, hope, activity, commitment; and they also express the cycles into which human beings fall, especially the valley times of anxiety and frustration. In addition we find that social programs are subject to a major problem to which creativity in individual lives is not vulnerable. It is that in social programs the integrative process that operates in individual lives is not as easily accessible. The fact that there are usually several persons involved in a social program means that the dialectical process of cycles moving toward integration is multiple, and is therefore complicated and often beset by difficulties. We continue to work on a social level to bring into existence social programs that require the participation of many individuals, knowing that participation of many persons has historically been a source of major frustration. It is at the root of the failure of most efforts to establish utopian communities in the past. We must assume that it would be a source of failure in the future as in the past.

There is a way, however, that we can work toward utopia in its fundamental sense of social hope without being subject to the vulnerabilities of the past. It is by developing in individuals the qualities of a Utopian Person. When these qualities are present in many individuals in a society, the fact that will follow by itself is that a utopian atmosphere will be established. It will be there in modern civilization as a matter of attitude even though the community itself will not have been reorganized on the outer level. But the frustrations and failures that have beset utopian societies in the past will thereby be avoided.

What are the qualities of Utopian Persons? The fundamental thing that we know is the process by which the experiences take place that lead an individual to become a Utopian Person. Basic is the fact of a time of discordance in the life causing the energies of the life to be blocked in their outer movement. The nature of life energies in human beings is to be constantly in motion. If they cannot move outward, they move inward. That is why the frustrations of outer life in individuals lead to a deepening of inner experience, sometimes disturbing dreams, and always images that lead to new life integrations at least on a symbolic level. Disharmonies in outer life lead to extended inner processes, the outcome of which can be a new and fuller view of life.

This is the fundamental characteristic of Utopian Persons. Having experienced disharmonies in life, their energies are forced into the depths of the psyche where they are brought into contact with symbolic realities that are universals of human existence in the sense that they apply to all human beings. When individuals are pushed to this depth in themselves by the pressures of their anxieties in the dialectics of life, the universals which they experience can give them a perspective of life that sets into context and resolves their personal conflicts. It gives them a larger vision. But this vision, while it expands their range of experience, also binds them to a view of life that includes all within its scope. Having been in contact with this depth of inner experience, they have touched the universals of life. From that point they cannot help but be Utopian Persons. After that inner experience they can no longer be happy with their own lot unless they feel that they are contributing to the lives of other human beings. For many individuals this experience inserts a substantial element of pain into their lives. But for civilization as a whole it is a great benefit. It means that there are some human beings who, whether by choice or because they are forced to by inner pressures, look at society not in terms of their own selfish desires but in terms of the needs of the whole. These are the Utopian Persons in every walk of life in the modern world.

We know now that the new world of mankind cannot be built on the basis of blueprints for idealized communities; it can come only out of the cumulative inner experience of individuals. There is an open point at the center of the tension of time in need of being filled both personally and socially. We feel the vacuum of it in our civilization. It can be filled creatively only out of the inner experience of individuals, person by person, each contributing a little bit out of his or her own depth. To open a road for many such experiences of diverse kinds so that many persons out of their personal travails can build cumulatively a prophetic vision of life is one of the important ways in which we may be able to rebuild civilization in the image of the human spirit.

It seems indeed that a new vision of man is coming into being and is seeking to establish itself in our world. We require it. We require it as an answer to the confusions and disturbances of our time in history and as an antidote for the breakdown in social meaning that has been diagnosed as personal neurosis. But most of all we require it as a means of establishing a connection with life that will enable us to reach into ourselves and into one another, to know love not as a doctrine but as a quality of our experience, and to recognize as a fact of our experience that there is actually a power that works through love, which is a transforming, a healing, a making whole of life.

For modern persons to participate in life at its dimension of inner depth is at the heart of this. It concerns a dimension of experience that is not commonly accessible in everyday life, but the awareness of this dimension, and the possibility of individuals developing the capacity of gaining access to it, is the essence of the new Image of Utopia that is called for and is being called forth in our time. It involves another way of experiencing our relation to life. This image of utopia is not to be brought into being by any organized program. Rather it comes about on the same level of the psyche where dreams happen, and in the same self-contained, integral way.

The new image of utopia is not to be found in outer symbols nor in any special set of symbols. It is an inner thing and cannot be put outside. And yet, this image, since it is an intimation of something that has been given ahead of time, must have a vehicle to carry it across time to enable it to become real in the world. It requires a vehicle to carry it from the point where it is an intimation on the dream level through the in-between times to the point where it can be established and lived and communicated in the world. Toward this end, symbols are necessary to serve as vehicles; but a special kind of symbol is required. It is not to be a representational symbol, a symbol that stands for something as a flag stands for one's country. It is not a symbol that refers to an external reality. But it must be an elemental symbol, a symbol that *is*, and lives, and works of itself. It must be a symbol that has an unfolding life of its own in which individual human beings can participate, and which can extend its life and theirs by means of their participation. There are some few symbols of this kind now in the world, but they are rare. They can only be valid and effective symbols for the Utopian task when they are open-ended, even as the psyche of a human being is open-ended.

At this time in history the primary need is for a doorway of initiation, a way of entry to the larger dimension of experience. Because of the poverty of symbols in our time, people require a new doorway that can serve as an entrance for them to the future image of reality of which their intimations tell them. The need is for no particular kind of door, but for the openness of doorways. To serve as such a doorway a symbol must be fresh, and alive; and its sources must be deep. Thus we reach out for living symbols that can be enacted in our personal existence. We require new visions and new, non-institutional meeting places that can serve as the social embodiment of the no-place, the *u-topia*, that is the depth of the soul. We require symbols that can be as present and as available for us as Jerusalem was for Meister Eckhart. We require symbol, things, and places that are real in the world and that also point beyond themselves. The vision of life contained in the image of utopia is one such living symbol. Utopian Persons feel it spontaneously from within themselves and are drawn to work toward it on the outer level. It is an image of life that sees all human beings developing as individuals as they draw on the resources in their private depths. It is an image of individuality, and it is also an image of society in a day to come.

P A R T   T W O

The Dialectic of the Creative Psyche:
Form, Time, and Opus
(Eranos, 1965)

13

The Opposites
of Inner and Outer:
The Making of Form

At this meeting I would like to explore with you a subject that I began here at Eranos two years ago, the dialectics of the *inner* and *outer* aspects of a human being's life.

There is in one sense something artificial in such a distinction. A person's life is not to be divided into fractions some of which are inward while others are outward, in the sense perhaps of some being spiritual while others are material; or in the further sense of some being subjective or symbolic while others are objective and literal. The life of a human being is experienced as a unity, both as inner and outer at the same time. To speak of "looking inward" or of being "inner directed" is after all a figure of speech, a metaphor of space applied to the psychological dimension of human life, where it can be very misleading. It is particularly misleading when we consider that it is the actions, the events, the living out of one's life in relationships—relationships which may be with other human beings or with non-human tasks, works to be done, land to be farmed, clay to be sculpted, a problem in science to be solved. All these are *enactments* of a person's life and they involve feelings and desires and insights which may be described as being *within* the individual.

The prime characteristic of these so-called *inner* factors is that they move outward in fulfilling themselves. They are *inner*, and yet their very nature draws them outside of themselves in order that they may be fulfilled. The idea, or the desire, or the intuition, requires something that will make it tangible; it needs to embody itself in a form, for then it can be felt to be real. Not only this, but when it is embodying itself in a form, it is extending itself; it is carrying forward the process of growth that is inherent in it. The idea or the image, therefore, whatever is perceived inwardly as a potentiality, necessarily moves forward into form as it enacts itself. In a sense it goes from the inner place of the psyche to an outer place in the environment surrounding it. But this is all a single process. The apparent dichotomy of inner and outer is thus a *unity in process*, a movement by which that which is a potentiality in the psyche extends itself and takes itself a step further into actuality, by filling itself out with the tangibility of form.

It is the process of this that we wish to study in some detail, especially in so far as it will enable us to see how the form of personal existence is brought into being. The building of the form of personal existence is the ultimate opus of individuality. It is a unitary process, but it has many phases and stages and cycles, and even an over-all spiraling effect. The dynamics of this is what we want to study, as much as we can here, to follow the process of personality formation from its appearance as a potentiality, through the struggles of its growth, ultimately to the various levels of its fulfillment, as it takes form in works out in the world and gradually builds the opus of personal existence within the individual.

Having brought out the point that there is a unity of process connecting what we speak of as inner and outer, we have to take note also of the fact that inner and outer are experienced psychologically as being opposites, and are experienced even as being actively in conflict with each other. This is how they are *felt* subjectively. It is an intuitive perception and, as intuitions often do, it reflects an organic process operating at a level more fundamental than consciousness. The core of this process is contained in the fact that the main impulses to action, especially those that are felt to be most integrally one's own, those that express the unique seed of one's potentiality, derive from within oneself. For that is where the seed of one's becoming is felt to be—within. But when they proceed, as it is their nature to do, to move out into the world to embody themselves in the reality of a form, the original image, which is the creative and propelling factor, encounters difficulties. What began on the inner level finds the obstacles to its unfoldment on the outer level.

The experience that is at the core of the process of psychological growth is the perception in life that the inner comes into conflict with the outer. From several points of view this is the basic dialectic of the human psyche, for it is the tension that arises out of this inherent opposition that draws the development of the individual onward. Being a dialectic, which means a confrontation of opposites in the actuality of life, a great deal depends upon the attitude that is taken in the midst of the conflict. If a rigid posture of opposition is adopted, the two sides of the dialectic may harden so that a constructive synthesis cannot be achieved. On the other hand, if a flexible attitude is established that makes possible a dialogue between the opposites, an outcome is possible in which it can truly be said that growth has taken place in the person. We shall want to inquire into the way of this.

It must be obvious at the outset that in speaking of the opposition of the inner and the outer, we have in mind a much larger realm of experience than the libidinal, instinctual drives as Freud described them. In that view, the conception is that the individual is thrusting outward in quest of pleasure by giving vent to energies that are basically sexual.

Conflict between inner and outer then occurs because the drive toward libidinal pleasure collides with the norms and prohibitions of the community. This is a basic concept underlying Freudian theory, the conflict between the individual and the authority of the community.

There is much more than this, however, involved in the dialectic of inner and outer as the core of the creative process of the psyche. In the first place, the drives that come from within, from what we speak of as the seed of the person, are much more specific and more meaningful in their content than mere libido. They contain tendencies toward specific social patterns of behavior, for man is indeed a social being, and the depths of the psyche are highly socialized, even in specific historical terms. Thus the social forms of the activities that are possible for an individual are already present in the seed of the psyche. The potential of being a poet or a soldier, a businessman or an engineer, a political leader or a healer of the spirit, is present in the individual from the very beginning. Whether they will be able to fulfill themselves and take outer form in the world is another question. But they are, in any case, the specific social potentials in the individual psyche. They are predispositions placed in the person by a combination of factors that are too numerous and really too elusive for us to attempt to define. We cannot say it is nothing but this or that. It is many things. In general, however, these tendencies of individual expression are what I have spoken of elsewhere as dynatypes. The main point to stress about them here is that, since they are formed within the seed of personality and since they emerge in the course of its growth, the individual's perception of them as expressions of his own unique selfness is that they come from within. They are the *inner*, and they are identified intuitively with one's true individuality.

On the other hand, as the person grows, especially during the years of childhood, he draws into himself attitudes and styles of life from other persons who are living close to him, from other individuals and from the social environment as a whole. It is as though he unconsciously mirrors the behavior of others, reflects it in himself, and enacts it as though it were his own. Thus, for example, the mannerisms of parents or teachers or friends, patterns of behavior which they follow, attitudes toward life, their styles of emotionality, anxieties which they may have, or enthusiasms, their religious devotions, their unconscious guilts, even the dynatype that is working toward expression in the other person may be reflected in one's self, as a child, for example, may be driven to live out the unfulfilled and even the unconscious ambitions of a parent.

We are all familiar in this respect with the young man who is drawn into the ministry or into a status profession like medicine because it is a wish his mother has. He may even believe that the desire is his own, so subtle and so unconscious is this process by which the environmentally derivative desire is reflected in one's self. We have also seen the situation of the young man who enters a field of work his father aspired to but could not attain, or who, also in unconscious obedience, enters the same profession, as though by so doing he would extend his father's life. Such vocations may be entered upon with the best intentions, but they often have the effect of diverting the individual from the sources of what could be his own integral development.

This mirroring quality of the psyche has the effect of drawing into the individual, as though they were his own, images of himself and of others, of his life, his goals, attitudes, styles, and habits of behavior that are not derived from his own seed. He takes them over from his social situation or from others related to him and he lives them as though they were his own, but they are not really him. He experiences them as *inner* because they work upon him as motivating forces from the inside, but actually they are not inner because their source is outside of him. They only seem to be within him because of this artificial mirroring effect of the psyche. And this is where the dialectic of inner and outer shows itself in most fundamental form, where that which is outer becomes something inner and acts as though it were inner, that is, acts as though it were the individual's own authentic nature.

The difference has important consequences, because an image of one's self and one's life that is rooted in the seed of one's self has the power to grow as a seed does. It is connected to a source of life and energy that replenishes itself and enlarges itself out of its own natural capacities. This is an organic process of life, that we readily perceive the fact in our lives that growth makes manifest capacities and energies which were only potentials before. Psychologically, then, it is possible for the individual to grow in his resources and powers when the primary image unfolding in him is rooted in the seed of his person. But if the image he is trying to live is a *reflected image* so that the reason he feels that it is within him is only because of the mirroring effect of the psyche, there is no possibility of authentic growth taking place.

This conception and the possibility of identifying it, of preceiving it and of being able to describe it specifically, is of tremendous practical importance. One of the great tasks psychologically is to be able to distinguish whether particular qualities are really potentials in a person or not. We may see an image there, but the question is whether the image which we see is merely a reflected image, or whether it is a seed image that is organically present in the person. Only in the latter case will it be able to grow. The image of a tree that we see reflected in a lake may attract us with great power. But the reflection does not have the capacity of growing. Only the tree itself can grow; and that out of its own true roots.

If we translate this metaphor into the terms of human life, we arrive at the fundamental question of identity, of being freed from the false starts and the false pressures of goals that would have us be what we are not. But to come into contact with our own identity is actually a very difficult achievement. For the greater part of their lives, human beings are living what they are not. They are living something that they call by their names. But to reach their own identity, to be in touch with one's seed, which is actually to make authentic growth possible for the person, requires a fundamental experience that may have a shaking impact. Psychologically it is an experience of initiation that is called for, initiation in the midst of life, and eventually initiation on a variety of existential levels. We shall return to this point in a little while.

14

Growth and the Life of the Spirit

First, however, let us take note of what is implied in the concept of psychological growth. In all the species of nature a process of growth takes place within the context and limitations of the potentialities of the particular species. The individual is capable of growth up to a certain point and within a general range of possibilities, give or take a little for variations of individuals and new adaptations. Man also is limited in the possibilities of his growth, but the range of variation in him is so great as to be virtually infinite. As the Talmudic story puts it, when God was creating man, He did not complete His task. He refrained from making man perfect, but left that as a task remaining to be done. He left it for man himself to do, specifically for man to achieve in his existence as an individual. The human being is therefore neither perfect nor complete according to his nature, as other, more limited species are. His life is open-ended in its possibilities, and this is precisely why man is the species that holds the possibility of carrying the evolution of life to further levels. It may indeed be that the reason for our feeling that there is a spiritual meaning to human existence comes essentially from this intimation, that the human species has within its integral nature the collective destiny of eventually carrying the evolution of life to a dimension greater than that on which man entered it.

There are none the less certain specific and relatively fixed stages of development through which the human individual must pass. The body matures in accordance with its necessary pattern of growth, and accompanying these physiological changes new emotional needs and capacities appear as well. For example, the relation to parents, dependency and the urge to personal freedom, the beginnings of affection, the attachment of individuals to one another, the beginnings of love, sexual love and the awareness of an ego emerging in oneself, a place in the world, a work to do, all these and many others are part of the normal development of individuals in all the cultures of the world. All these, both physiologically and psychologically are necessary phases of growth inherent in the species, and therefore they are essentially predictable and can be described in advance.

There comes a point, however, when the ego has grown strong enough, where individuality rises past its predictable patterns to moments of creative insight and enlarged awareness. These are the moments that are breakthroughs in time when something new enters the world casting its light ahead of itself. Whenever such an event occurs it comes by means of an individual, but the collective life of the species as well as the possibilities of experience of the individuals within the species are different forever afterward. These are the acts of discovery, of knowledge in science or in technology, acts of creativity in art or poetry or literature, acts of inspiration in religion or prophecy, and the leadership of nations. They include also on a more private, less conspicuous level, acts of love between persons, the occasional agape that breaks through the walls of individuality so that dialogue at the depth of being becomes a reality.

What I am indicating is this, that the necessary development of the human species takes the individual to a level where it requires him to make a leap beyond himself. He has to do this as a member of the species in order to fill in the open-ended possibilities of human existence; and also as an individual in order that he may discover the meaning of his personal existence. The fact is that the human being creates the meaning of his existence in the act of living it; afterwards, but only afterwards, he can look back and discover what the meaning of his life is.

In his psychological development, a human being grows by natural stages organically, until with physical maturation he comes to a plateau. He may remain at this plateau functioning within the terms that his culture prescribes, and within its framework he may live out his days more or less contentedly. But if the impulse to further growth is pressing within him, he cannot possibly be content to remain there. Then he may live on this plateau and use it as his base, in order to launch some further movement in his life. This may be in some particular area of his experience, a small area or a large area depending on his capacities. From this plateau he may thrust forward in a creative act of individuality, and with this personal experience of his, a new insight or a new emotion, an act of leadership or an act of love will be brought into the world.

These creative acts of persons are their individual leaps upward and beyond the plateau on which they merely exist biologically and socially as human beings. Often an individual has just one brief moment in which he leaps off the plateau, a brief moment of insight, of vision, a momentary act of dedication or of love, and then he drops back onto the plateau and remains there. But in that leap he has touched something. That which has transpired was a moment of creation in which something new was brought into the totality of all human existence so that it remains forever afterward as a fact. Afterwards it is an element in the future experience of individuals in the species. The reality of that creative moment lives on, whether or not it was given tangible form in words or in color or in sound as a poem or a painting or perhaps a melody. The immortality of what has been created does not depend on the outward form it takes. It depends rather on the authenticity of the experience, on its inward integrity, its unself-conscious spontaneity, and on the power that derives from all of these. For in that moment, something elusive and intangible but nontheless real has been brought into the world.

These creative events are meanings that did not exist before they happened; but once they have happened, they exist forever. They occur as the experiences of individuals and they give meaning to the lives of the individuals in whom they take place; they also become the raw materials of the inner lives of the persons who are outside of the original experiences but who absorb them and share in their emotions. Seen from one side, these experiences constitute the meaning of the life of the individual through whom they were brought into existence; but they are not contained by the individual. They may mean everything to him, but the person who created them is merely the instrument of what has been created, whether it was a great poem, or a spontaneous and unrecorded moment of devotion or love. The individual does not possess these moments. Once they have been created, they exist on their own. They go out and reach beyond the individual. Collectively they build and then participate in something more than him. The collectivity and continuity of cummulative moments which are experienced by persons as individuals become a total human inheritance and possession. They belong then to everyone, and may be shared in and drawn upon by all, especially by those individuals who have the greatest sensitivity by reason of experiences they themselves have known. This is particularly true with respect to individuals who find themselves moved by similar images in the seed of their psychological being. Because of the cohering principle which these images provide, a great community of knowing and unspoken communication can then take place within such groups, groups that have no formal bond beyond the sharing of equivalent experiences and recognitions of reality.

What is being shared in then is as a great sea or a great atmosphere in which individuals of particular levels of experience live and move and have their being. Just as fish live within the atmosphere of the sea and are both encompassed by it and sustained by it, and as human beings live within an atmosphere of air on what we have spoken of as the plateau of ordinary social life, so it is that individuals who are moved by a common image at the depth of themselves, and who have glimpsed its reality in the creative act of even a momentary recognition, participate in an atmosphere that is as the sea to them in that it contains them and sustains them. It provides the atmosphere, the content of meaning for their lives, and it provides a vibrant, ever-moving source of new meanings. In this sense, the individual events that comprise these creative moments of vision and love become as the drops of water which form the bays and the seas and the oceans and give them their distinctive composition and their flavor. They become the atmosphere and the resource of particular groups of persons, artists, religions, nations, and ultimately mankind.

Now, to recapitulate this thought. Human beings develop to a certain point physiologically and psychologically as part of the organic requirements of the species. They then come safely to rest upon a social plateau on which they can remain or from which they are forced to leap by an inner urging. These leaps then become the meaning of the individual's life; and the accumulation of these leaps comprise the special addition to the process of natural evolution which is mankind's unique contribution extending the movement and the meaning of life. Not knowing what else to call it, we may call this the spiritual destiny of mankind. And for the individual who consciously participates in this, lacking other terms, we may call it the life of the spirit.

While we speak of this as spirit, there is also another language we can use, the language of psychology. At the present time there are a variety of psychological theories being offered as attempts to interpret man's life, to explain his so-called "normal functioning", and to provide therapeutic treatment when his behavior becomes disturbed. Many of these theories vary from one another so widely not only in orientation but also in content, in the very subjects that are studied, that it must often seem to the outsider that the field of psychology is a modern Tower of Babel. It may well be, however, that the psychological babbling during this past generation has been working in the direction of a perspective by which it is being made possible for us to see what the discipline of psychology needs to achieve for modern man. We may now be able to see what modern man needs psychology *for*, and from that draw our criteria of what the discipline of psychology ought to be.

The line of thinking we have been following may provide us with such a perspective. There is an inherent process of development in man as in other species leading to the plateau of normalcy. For each there is a certain possibility that may be attained. But man is distinguished from other species in that when his basic development has been completed the important potentials of his life just begin. The psychological growth of man leads him to creative acts that have unpredictable spiritual as well as evolutionary effects. The task of psychology, then, is to study the factors that provide both the necessity and the resources for those acts of self-transforming growth by which man creates new meanings for his existence.

This process of growth in man is open-ended in its potentials, but these potentials often remain dormant in the unopened depths of personality. What is required, then, is not a psychiatry to diagnose man for his weaknesses, but a perspective and a method to draw forth the process of growth in him and thus build his capacity for self-transforming creative acts. In my experience, I have found the conception to be validated again and again that where there are anxieties or other disturbances of personality to be healed, the best therapy is provided not by analysis of the symptoms but by entering into the process of growth in the person, stimulating it, strengthening it, until one has awakened the recognition in the individual that the process of growth is not an abstraction but is the most operative reality of his inner being. The way to therapy, in other words, is to be found not by analyzing the psyche but by evoking it and drawing it to a further level of development within the context and in the terms of the potentials of the individual's life.

The seeming paradox that has often been shown during the past generation to be a significant fact of personality is that when therapy is achieved by the evoking of the growth process, it leads far beyond the plateau of normalcy, and opens vistas not presented at all in the original problem. Psychological healing then becomes an event of spiritual proportions. That is why a psychology conceived in terms of the process of growth in man and directed toward evoking what is latent in the depths of the person holds the possibility of contributing much more even than restoring "normalcy" to the life of individuals. Such a psychology holds the possibility of becoming the instrument by which a power of spirit is awakened in modern man enabling him to take the next step that is called for in human development.

We come then to the question of an approach that can help us both in understanding and in evoking the process of growth in human beings. This double purpose, I should point out, indicates an important way in which depth psychology is different from other branches of science. For other sciences it is sufficient to obtain an objective knowledge of the subject matter, which may be applied or adapted in useful ways, as for example, the way the technological and industrial arts have used the discoveries in chemistry and biology. But neither chemistry, nor biology, nor physics, have any desire to alter the basic subject matter which they are studying.

Depth psychology does, however, wish to have a direct effect on its subject matter; in fact that is the reason for which it has been brought into existence. Depth psychology was brought into being in nineteenth-century Europe essentially because the quality of behavior and the quality of consciousness of modern man had become disturbed and needed to be healed—or, as was later discovered, the consciousness of modern man needed to be transformed. On the assumption that modern man needed to be healed, depth psychology began as a form of therapy based on diagnosis in terms of a conception of psychological pathology. The first model which depth psychology followed was drawn from the medical arts. Experience during the past generation has increasingly shown, however, that modern man's need is not to be healed; that is, his problem is not primarily a medical problem. But modern man's need is that he be transformed with respect to the quality of his consciousness, that he be enabled to move to a further level of development with respect to the interior aspect of his life. This poses problems and has requirements of quite a different kind from scientific analysis or medical treatment in terms of pathology.

It means that the very concepts that are used in thinking about the subject matter will affect it, will either alter it, or rigidify it. The author who observed this fact and first commented on it was Otto Rank.* Rank had observed both Freud

---

*Progoff, Ira, *The Death and Rebirth of Psychology*, Crown/McGraw Hill, New York, 1956, Chapter VIII.

and Adler very closely, and he had studied Jung in a not un-sympathetic way. He noted that as these pioneer thinkers for-mulated their concepts, which were intended originally as objective descriptions of psychological facts, the concepts were immediately seized upon as doctrines or as beliefs and they immediately had a therapeutic effect. They may have been affirmative or negative, but they had a direct effect upon the psychological conduct of the persons who read their books. And this effect was quite independent of the objective scientific validity of the statements being made by Freud, Adler, Jung, and the others.

This observation led to the inference that the way the psychoanalytical movement was developing marked it as being not so much a science as an ideology. On this point, Rank went further to state, that in order to maintain the status of psychology as a branch of science, it is necessary to take account of its ideological quality by noting the distinc-tion between psychological statements that are made as the-ory and psychological statements that are made for the purpose of therapy. In making this point, Rank was, I think not intentionally, working to restore the original model of depth psychology as a branch of medicine dealing with the pathology of human behavior. But this, as events have turned out, could not be done because the model was not appropri-ate for the particular need that depth psychology has to meet. If the distinction that Rank made between theory and therapy could be maintained in practice it would mean that theoretical statements would be tested by a criterion of scien-tific objectivity, in the same way that statements made in a biology laboratory are tested objectively. Then as therapy they would be applied in the manner of the medical practi-tioner who is permitted as an artist in his field to use his intuition, his bedside manner, tender loving care, and other subjectivities in order to bring about a cure.

Anyone who was observed the varieties of depth psychology in practice cannot fail to notice, however, that this distinction between theory and therapy is purely theoretical. It does not hold up in practice, and this means that the theory is not valid. The very style in which a psychological concept is formulated shapes the quality of consciousness of the person who hears and accepts it. Think, for example, of how the mentality of a person is affected by the fact of his being given a Freudian formulation of his psychological problem in terms of infantile sexuality and repressed hatred of the parents; or how it is affected by a Jungian formulation in terms of archetypes and individuation; or by an Adlerian formulation in terms of inferiority feelings and *Gemeinshaftsgefuhl.* Each has its own ideological effect, as others do as well. The formulation of the concept stirs up and alters the quality of the consciousness that it was attempting to describe.

This situation should not be deplored; it needs merely to be recognized as a fact. Actually it opens very constructive possibilities which should be considered seriously. The need of modern man that originally called depth psychology into existence involved disturbances in behavior which, we have since discovered, cannot be basically overcome until the quality of modern consciousness has been changed. Modern man, as we have said, does not need to be healed; he needs to have the quality of his consciousness enlarged in ways that can alter the atmosphere and content of the worldwide civilization in which we are all now living. There is indeed the possibility that depth psychology, in its new developments, can become the instrument by which this need can be met. But it will need to have a clear awareness of the effects of its formulations on its subjects.

In this context, we may speak of two general types of sciences. There are the *declarative sciences* which seek to make objective statements about a specific subject, verifying these statements within a fixed frame of reference; and there are what we may call the *evocative sciences,* of which depth psychology is for us a prime example, but in which we would include also several other areas of the study of man. These are sciences in which the manner of study and the style of formulation in itself affects the subject matter in an active way. These are sciences also that seek and whose nature forces them to reach out always beyond themselves, especially by stirring up and eventually changing the student. For the main quality of these *evocative sciences* is that their primary subject of study and the primary object of the transformation that they seek is the life and quality of consciousness of the student himself.

Let us begin then with an awareness of depth psychology as an *evocative science,* one whose very formulations stir up and change the subject being studied, which is oneself and one's fellow human being. Knowing then that our concepts have consequences, we must be very careful in their use. They can have an effect that is either affirmative or negative; and unfortunately it is very difficult to know in advance which the effect will be. Therefore, the best principle seems to be to work with an economy of concepts, using as few as is feasible, and making those few as neutral as possible in their formulation. The one other principle, in addition to working with a minimum of concepts that are neutral or at least non-prejudicial in their format, is that the style of working should have the effect of stirring up the psychological processes of those who are studying the subject, thus drawing the students ever closer to themselves by deepening the tone and level of their inner experience. This is probably best achieved by bringing about an intensity of involvement on the part of the students. In this regard, I have found in teaching depth psychology at the university level that one cannot handle it as a description of subject matter as in philosophy or as a statement of theoretical principles. It is necessary rather to draw the student into it with material from his own life. Then eventually he will be able to recognize what the process is because he will have touched and felt it in himself. Whether it is perceived as a science or as an art, depth psychology is *not declarative but evocative* in its tone and style.*

---

*See Appendix p. 263

15

The Times
of a Life

We can now return to our question of what psycholocigal approach is most appropriate for understanding and evoking the process of growth in modern man. We wish to avoid concepts that will have an ideological effect, and therefore it seems best to come to the other human being just as we find him or her, avoiding any prior theories or *a priori* concepts. Some working tools are necessary, however, and at Drew University, where we have been conducting a continuing research into the creative process of personality, we have devised a basic format which I would like to describe to you as a foundation for our further comments.

When we choose an individual as a subject of study to investigate the creative process of personality—let us say some well-known person of a past generation—we begin by making a chronological listing of all the facts that may possibly be relevant for understanding his psychological development. This is intended merely as a neutral work of fact gathering; but its effect may not be nearly as neutral as it seems, since modern western thinking has developed an historicizing bias based on the loose presupposition that if one psychological event has preceded another it must therefore be the cause of it. This attitude has been particularly prevalent wherever there has been an analytical or reductive approach to psychology. But we merely begin by making our chronological listing as a fact-gathering enterprise, and we make no interpretations at that point.

We then carry our chronological approach one step further by dividing the individual's life into seven roughly defined but basic periods, or time-stages. These are:

T-1 The period covering roughly the first ten years of life.

T-2 Ages 11–15 approximately, or the years of early adolescence.

T-3 Ages 16–20 approximately, or the latter part of adolescence.

T-4 Ages 20–30. The beginnings of maturity in which the lines of family and work are laid down.

T-5 Ages 31–45, or approximately the early middle years when the most active period of work takes place.

T-6 Ages 46–60, or approximately the later middle years, the time of ripening maturity.

T-7 The years after sixty which may be a declining time in some cultures but is being extended and enlarged in modern times.*

In filling in these divisions we begin to be selective since we are trying to narrow down the possibilities of the psychologically dynamic factors. The specific contents which we discern here are mostly such as can be recognized and described because of the discussions that have appeared in any of the varieties of psychological literature. At this point, we are

*See Appendix p. 255

being as widely inclusive as possible and are still attempting to restrain ourselves from drawing any conclusions. We are, however, beginning to narrow the focus of our study of the individual. As we draw our information together, certain patterns begin to emerge. In particular, we discover that the development of personality through these stages of life moves in the direction of an experience of initiation, both a primary experience of initiation to life and successive initiations to larger dimensions of awareness. These experiences are the key to the emergence of form and meaning in individual existence. In order to appreciate what is involved in them, let us look in somewhat greater detail at the first four time-stages of which we have spoken.

The first stage, which covers the period of childhood approximately to the tenth year, certainly plays a very important role in the development of personality. There is increasing evidence, however, that the role of this period has been greatly overemphasized in recent psychological interpretations. Psychoanalytic theory in particular has concentrated its attention on the early years of childhood as the time when the basic patterns of behavior are formed. In its analytic treatment it looks back into this early period in quest of the *causes* of later personality syndromes. But there is little validation for the assumption that the later developments of the personality are *caused* in childhood. We are warranted in making nothing more than the neutral statement that childhood is the beginning of the human experience of growth and that, depending upon the individual case, it casts a larger or a smaller shadow over the years of maturity that follow it.

To study the years of childhood reductively looking for the origins of personality is not nearly as fruitful as studying that period from a prospective point of view. Those are the years when the process of growth gets into motion. There is, therefore, the greatest value in being able to see how the momentum of growth is generated in the early years of life. Early experiences, early memories, and especially recurrent images and dreams drawn from that period of life are of the greatest value in this connection. They are like harbingers of spring that carry the promise of buds that will open when their time for ripening arrives, and that indicate also the style and tempo, and perhaps the difficulties, with which development will take place. These images and memories thus give us an entry to the process of growth which expresses itself in the human psyche just as it does in the world of nature.

Of particular significance in this regard are those experiences in the early years of life that are recalled with great emotional intensity and are not forgotten even in the later years of maturity. In his practice Alfred Adler always made it a point to ask his patients to tell him the earliest memories they could recall. He felt that these gave him a clue to the subjective style and the inner principle by which the individual's life was unfolding. We find also that such memories often bring considerable light to our understanding of the lives of creative persons.

An experience of Abraham Lincoln which we discussed at Eranos last year is an excellent instance of this. It concerns a memory that Lincoln recalled in his later years reminding him of the time when, as a very small boy, he helped his father plant the seeds in a newly cultivated field. The family had just completed another move farther out to the edge of the frontier, and his father had invested much labor in making the virgin soil fit for planting. All day they had worked, his father preceding him with grain seed while the small boy followed with pumpkin seed. At length the day's work was done, and Lincoln's memory was of his standing with his father in the doorway of their log cabin watching the rain

come down in torrents and wash away the seeds they had so
laboriously planted.

In recalling it, Lincoln felt the incident to be indicative of
a recurrent quality of his life. He regarded it as a keynote to
his destiny in that he was convinced through all his formative
years that this would be a characteristic of his life. Things
would always come hard for him. If he planted seeds, the
rain would wash them away; if he became President of the
United States, it would be at a time when a united country
was no longer in existence so that the honors of the presi-
dency would be washed away in the painful conduct of a civil
war.

Memories of this type are important not because they are
causative, but because they reflect the inner style of the personality. The intensity of emotion with which they are remembered is itself indicative of the fact that they express a
fundamental quality of the individual. That is indeed the reason why they are remembered, and it is also the reason why
they are of value in understanding and in tracing the growth
principles of personality.

The second chronological stage of which we have spoken,
covering approximately the years from eleven to fifteen, is the
period of early adolescence. It is important primarily as the
time when the process of growth has proceeded far enough
to bring forth the first strong sense of individual identity. The
young person becomes aware then of his own existence as
distinct from that of the rest of the world; and with this also,
with the dawning religious sensitivity of youth, a new kind of
connection to the world opens.

An incident that C. G. Jung relates in his *Memories,
Dreams, and Reflections* is a poignant and meaningful instance of this. As a boy at about the beginning of this age
period, Jung had a favorite stone on which he would sit when
he was alone. He tells how he became familiar with it, identified himself with it, and at length found himself posing this

interesting question: "Am I the one who is sitting on the stone, or am I the stone on which *he* is sitting?*" It recalls a similar question raised twenty-three centuries earlier by the Taoist philosopher Kwang Tse who asked: "Am I Kwang Tse dreaming he is a butterfly, or am I the butterfly dreaming he is Kwang Tse?"

The question of identity opens in two directions. On the one hand there is the necessity for a strong and clear sense of one's own individuality, one's ego, independence, and distinctness in relation to others. But with it there comes also the realization of the individuality of others, and of an existence in others that is both separate from us and intimately connected to us. In the early experience of Jung upon the rock both of these aspects are expressed, perhaps in an especially fragile way, because the sense of identity itself was still so young and tender. But this makes it all the more meaningful to note the similarity between the boy's question and the question posed so much more consciously by the sophisticated Chinese philosopher.

In pre-modern cultures the question of identity is raised in quite another way at this second chronological period of life. Here, at the time of early adolescence, identity is defined in terms of the individual's position in the community as a whole. Identity becomes a question of the social group to which one belongs, and at this age it becomes primarily a question of whether one is a child or an adult. Clearly this is the issue which defines the period of adolescence in every culture, for it is distinctively the period in the individual's existence when the transition into adult life is made. Adolescence, therefore, has this characteristic in the modern world as well, but its format is different in the tradition-bound cultures of the past.

---

*Jung, C.G., *Memories, Dreams, Reflections* (recorded and edited by Aniella Jaffe), Pantheon, N.Y., 1963.

Essentially there are three main types of factors which govern each of the stages of life. These are: the *biological*, the *cultural*, and the *existential*. The *biological* involves the physical development of the individual and the corresponding emotional changes that bring forth new needs as the life-process matures. The *cultural* concerns the social contexts in which the development of the individual takes place, and especially the outer framework of meaning for life-activities. The *existential* involves the *inner* framework of meaning and the unfoldment of the personal destiny of the individual.

We might suppose that the biological factors would remain constant and would provide an unchanging frame of reference for the process as a whole. This is not the case, however. Cultural factors exert a very great influence even upon the tempo of physical development, speeding it up or slowing it down, so that even the biological aspects of the life stages vary with the social situation. This is true especially of areas of life that relate to adolescence; but it is true of later phases, especially of maturation and the aging process as well. From the point of view of a holistic depth psychology, this phenomenon of the culturalization of the biological processes of individual growth, merits major attention in future research.*

Whereas in earlier cultures this was a time for launching out in life, in modern culture it can be no more than a time of waiting. Biologically, the energies are high, but the culture forces them to remain in abeyance, and thus they cannot develop until a later time. Their passage into adulthood is held up and postponed, thus enforcing a damming-up of life energies, and this, in turn, creates a great restlessness

---

*To my knowledge the psychological author who has made the greatest contribution to this subject is Otto Rank. Certainly it is Rank who has had the greatest effect on my own thinking in this regard. See especially Ernest Becker, *The Denial of Death*, The Free Press, New York, 1973 and Ira Progoff, *The Death and Rebirth of Psychology*.

of personality. In the modern world this is an in-between time. The best that one can hope for is that it will be a neutral time with no disruptive effects. It is a time of treading water in life, a time when there are large amounts of energy available to be expended, but the doors are closed on them. It is the uncomfortable time, as Hermann Hesse has said, of "the child who is no longer a child."* It is an unpleasant time, like the enforced holding of one's breath; and socially, for the early adolescent group as a whole, it is a situation of psychological vacuum. When there is a vacuum, however, the vacuum must be filled; and this may be the fundamental reason why the time of early adolescence is filled with foolish fads and irrational behavior in all those modern countries where the income level is high enough to support the search for fads.

The psychological vacuum that characterized this period of life may, however, also have a much more constructive effect. Because of its emptiness it is also a time of searching and of reaching out. It is the time when the sensitive adolescent actively begins to form an image of what he can possibly become when his energies will have been freed to enter the world. These years may then be a time in which there is a heightened awareness. The intense experiences that occur at this time can have profound and lasting effects. Quite in contrast to the psychoanalytic emphasis on infancy, the deep and shaking encounters that occur in early adolescence may have a much greater impact on the form that the personality finally takes than the so-called repressions of earlier years. A good instance of this was the experience of the great Quaker philosopher Rufus Jones. In his eleventh year, a serious illness brought him close to death. He survived it, and when he did he emerged with a sense of calling and a feeling of meaning

---

*Hesse, Hermann, Demian, Peter Owen, Vision Press, London, 1958, translated by W. J. Strachan. P. 53

in his life. It is interesting to note, however, that even Rufus Jones, being a person in the modern world, had to experience the rhythms and requirements of slow maturation as it is in modern culture. He had to wait until the later years of his life for his initiation into the hard realities of spiritual knowledge to take place.*

---

*Vining, Elizabeth Gray, *Friend of Life, The Biography of Rufus M. Jones*, Lippincott, New York, 1958.

16

Modern Culture
and the Psychology
of Initiation

The third stage of chronological growth is that of later adolescence covering roughly the years from sixteen to twenty. This is the time when the first and basic initiation into adult life should take place. In the modern world particularly, it is a critical time. It is the time when the old self of childhood dies and the new self, which is really the seed out of which the personal destiny of the individual will unfold in the course of adulthood, is brought into existence. It is essential that this transition take place, and the period of later adolescence is the phase of individual development that is the most appropriate time. Naturally, however, it does not always happen in the way that it should. In fact, the tendency in modern times is that this basic initiation does not take place until later years.

If the initiation to life does not take place at this time, the individual continues to live in an in-between world, one foot still in the world of childhood and the other foot tentatively dipping its toes from time to time in the rivers of adulthood. Many people in modern society, as we often have occasion to observe, live into the later years of their lives without undergoing the initiatory experience that makes the transition for them into adult awareness. This is why so much of modern

behavior and modern attitudes, as the style of the appeals in
the advertising media indicate, are on a quasi-adolescent
level. That is why this is often experienced as an era of inade-
quacy among men and of confusion among women. An essential ingredient for life, a certain quality of awareness, a
perspective, a stability, and an inward power, are lacking
until this initiation takes place. The possibility of living one's
authentic existence is held back and must wait until it
happens.

Whenever it takes place, whether in the life of a modern
individual or of a person living in any other period of history,
the initiation into adult existence follows the format of rites
that are found not only in the religions of primitive cultures,
but throughout the history of the advanced religions as well.
A basic cycle is involved, the cycle of a death and a transformed consciousness renewed in a new birth. In primitive
rituals the death is a symbolic death, which is, however, dramatized so intensely in the ceremonials that the individual
experiences it as the reality of his life. The death then seems
to be an imminent possibility, and it seems indeed that unless the reality of the death is experienced with sufficient intensity, it does not have the necessary initiatory effect.

An example of this is the primitive ceremony in which the
young man is held quite close to a fire, roasted, and toasted
for a full twenty-four hours at which time he is treated cere-
monially as though he were dead; and indeed he may come
quite close to death under such circumstances. The women
in the tribe then mourn him as dead, considering that the
child whom they had the responsibility of nurturing is no
longer alive for them. The men of the tribe then continue the
ceremony, offering the young man up to their god and beg-
ging a new life for him. This new life is the life of adulthood
in the tribe, as a warrior, as a hunter and, in sum, as an adult
male individual. This death, which he experiences as much

more than a symbol but as an actual possibility, is his initiation to life.

Dramatic rituals of this kind seldom occur in the modern situation. The closest we come to them is perhaps to be found in the prototypal events of the great Biblical religions, in so far as these are still experienced intensely enough to seem real. In the Judaic tradition, the theme is embodied in the events of the Mosaic exodus: the years of servitude, the conflict with Pharaoh, the flight from the land of bondage amidst suffering so great that death was an ever-present possibility; and ultimately the promise of redemption in the land of milk and honey. This set of historical events is recapitulated ritually each year in the Passover service. It clearly dramatizes the basic cycle of initiation: the death with its dangers and sufferings, and the rebirth with its new meaning for existence. Its limitation, however, is that its ancient symbolism now evokes a much smaller emotional response in the modern world than it did in more traditional periods. It becomes increasingly difficult, therefore, for modern individuals to identify the problems of their personal existence with the Exodus event, and the symbol becomes less and less capable of serving as a vehicle for the experience of initiation to life.

Drawn also from the same Biblical tradition but retaining a somewhat greater force in the modern world is the historical and eternal event of the death of Jesus on the cross. The essential cycle of initiation is enacted in it: the death in the midst of great suffering and the miraculous rebirth in fulfillment of a prophecy. The prototype of the cycle is contained here, the death of the old self with its restricted consciousness that ties one to childhood, and the birth of a new being which embodies immortality and personifies the emergence of a new meaning in existence. Even in the midst of the modern rationalistic era, many persons have continued to find that their inner perception of this event carries them through a personal transformation, a *conversion* of the old self into a new being capable of participating in life in terms of a larger dimension of awareness.

This is the working of the basic Christian image as a symbolic vehicle for the experience of initiation. Its value, however, is felt largely in terms of doctrinal beliefs and of assurances of faith which give the individual a feeling of belonging to the spiritual universe at large. As the symbolic event is ritually re-experienced in its appropriate ceremonial, it re-establishes the connection with the original timeless event of the death and rebirth. Each time it is enacted, it is experienced anew, and the reality of the connection is renewed.

These experiences are of great value in so far as they have the effect of drawing the individual's consciousness into the large perspective of an encompassing religious symbol like the death and rebirth of Jesus. The weakness and limitation of such experiences are found however in the fact that the experience of reality which they provide is not in terms of the specifics of the individual's own life. It may well be that in pre-modern cultures, when life followed traditional patterns and typologies, it was sufficient for the initiatory experience to come by means of a non-personal religious image; but in modern culture the uniqueness of the individual's existence has been so intensified that it is necessary for his religious experiences to emerge out of the very tissue and content of his individual life. Without this the traditional images are too hollow, and this is one reason that whatever faith is established in them by means of ceremonials must constantly be bolstered again and again through ritual repetition.

Since they are traditional rather than personal, cultural initiations to life do not carry with them the integrity and the indigenous power of the individual's unique life; and yet this is essential if they are to provide the new strength and meaning that are necessary for his existence. We should not be surprised to find, therefore, that the social format of the initiatory experience is changing in modern times and that it is appearing with new characteristics. One main aspect of this is the fact that the symbols of initiation and the experience of them are no longer primarily traditional or cultural, but are drawn from the dreams and life events of the individual's own existence. With this, lacking the cultural supports of tradition, the individual's path of initiation becomes much more difficult, uncertain, and often exceedingly lonely. None the less, this is the style in which the psychological experience of initiation is increasingly taking place in modern times, replacing the traditional rituals of the past.

We can see instances of this in many modern novels that deal with the search for meaning among adolescents. A particularly instructive example of this is the best-selling American novel, *Franny and Zooey* by J.D. Salinger*. There, attention is focused on young people of college age, especially those who are living in an atmosphere of modern cynicism which requires of them that they adopt a sophisticated attitude at least as their social pose. Salinger deals with the soft underside of this sophistication, showing how the psyche of the young person reaches toward authenticity even in the midst of the most superficial social values.

The central character in the novel is Franny, a college girl of good intelligence and cosmopolitan tastes. She has a boy friend, goes to football games, studies dramatics, dabbles in literature, and, more important than anything to her, she seeks a friendship and a belief that will be of lasting value. In the course of this search, she becomes interested in the mystical tract, *The Way of a Pilgrim*, in which a Russian peasant describes his search for a method of achieving unity with God. He walks all over Russia seeking this, asking whomever

---

*Salinger, J. D., *Franny and Zooey*, Little Brown and Co., 1961.

he meets, until he finally discovers and perfects through his own discipline the method of 'praying without ceasing'. This method involves the constant repetition of the phrase, 'Lord Jesus Christ have mercy on me'. The phrase is to be repeated continuously, at first verbally, and then eventually on subverbal levels until it becomes as natural and as unself-conscious as the flow of one's blood. At that point, the teaching promises, the repetition of the prayer will have so marked a spiritual effect that the quality of the individual's consciousness will be transformed.

Franny is much impressed by the pilgrim's conception, and she attempts to practice the method herself. She repeats the phrase endlessly under her breath as though with a religious dedication. When, however, she attempts to describe to her boyfriend what she understands herself to be doing in her practice of the method it becomes apparent that she is thinking of it not religiously but objectively as a psychological procedure. Although she has entered into the exercise with great emotion and spiritual desire, the name of God which the Pilgrim used and which she repeats, has only an intellectual meaning for her. She explains to her friend that it would be equally valid to say in place of the phrase, "Lord Jesus Christ", the phrase "Namu Amida Butsu" as in the Nembutsu sects of Buddhism, or "Om" as in Hinduism, or simply the word *God* as *The Cloud of Unknowing* recommends. Thus, all being equal to her, none has the intense personal effect that is necessary. In the midst of a crisis of personal confusion, she repeats the prayer as the Pilgrim suggested in an effort to save herself, but it does not work. She loses consciousness while automatically repeating the words: "Lord Jesus Christ have mercy on me."

At this point Salinger shifts the emphasis of his story. He introduces the reader to Franny's family, her mother and brother, and enables us to enter into the continuity of her life development with its aspirations and its impasses, all that had led her to the situation in which a new breakthrough of meaning became urgently necessary. He takes us then into Franny's inward world where a nightmarish dream reflects the disturbed condition in which her search is taking place*.

In the dream Franny was diving repeatedly into a swimming pool in an effort to come up with a special object lying on the bottom. The object itself was a ridiculous and seemingly inappropriate thing, a can of coffee, but in the dream this was the symbol that represented the goal of her searchings. She called out for others who were at the side of the pool, to come in also and to search with her. "You have your bathing suits on", she called out to them. "Why don't you do a little diving too?" But instead of diving in to assist her in her search, they only harassed her by trying to hit her with an oar each time she came to the surface after a fruitless dive into the depths. One other person was in the pool with her, a professor of comparative religion. But he was the most exasperating person of all. He simply stood in the water as an inactive observer, smiling and doing absolutely nothing.

Franny could only describe the dream as nightmarish because its atmosphere was deadening in its discouragement. The dream led her to the conclusion that no one in the intellectual environment to which she turned for support, not her university teachers and not her fellow students, would be helpful or even sympathetic to her. She was thrown back upon herself, being returned both to the darkness of her despair and to the confusion of what seemed to be an inevitably fruitless search. The dream showed her that help would not come from the outside, and thus it pressed her deeper into her own life.

Her conversations with her mother and her brother continued, but these also seemed to be circular and pointless. They were, however, the only real contacts with life that

*Ibid., p. 125–128

were available to her. These members of her family were the only persons in the world who had shared her life and with whom she could truly discuss it, difficult though these discussions might be. But no light seemed to be coming from this quarter either.

The outlook seemed unalterably black when an unexpected phone call came from her brother. He spoke to her now with a directness and honesty that was possible only because of their joint involvement in the earlier events of their lives, their participation in a difficult family enterprise, and their still unresolved mourning of a much beloved brother who had died. In the course of the discussion, the brother made a point which spoke to her deeply and suddenly awakened a new awareness in her. All the people in the world, all the people whom she had previously regarded merely as strangers, as an anonymous audience to her life, all of them were divine, all of them were the Christ. The statement came to her as a shaking insight and filled her with joy. And then abruptly her brother stopped their phone conversation, said, "I can't talk any more", and hung up.

Salinger's brief description of what followed is rich with suggestive implications. After her brother had hung up, Salinger writes, "Franny took in her breath slightly but continued to hold the phone to her ear. A dial tone, of course, followed the formal break in the conversation. She appeared to find it extraordinarily beautiful to listen to, rather as if it were the best possible substitute for the primordial silence itself. But she seemed to know, too, when to stop listening to it, as if all of what little or much wisdom there is in the world were suddenly hers. When she had replaced the phone, she seemed to know just what to do next, too. She cleared away the smoking things, then drew back the cotton bedspread from the bed she had been sitting on, took off her slippers, and got into the bed.

For some minutes, before she fell into a deep, dreamless sleep, she just lay quiet, smiling at the ceiling."*

We are left to conclude that the inward struggle through which Franny had been passing was resolved by this new insight, and by her experience of the primordial silence in the symbolic form of a dial tone. There is indeed good reason to feel that it would have that effect. The entire cycle of events, the confusion, the emotional breakdown, and the new realization from the telephone conversation and the way in which it ended, all followed the pattern of an initiation experience; and an initiation into life was the unconscious goal behind the turmoil through which Franny had been suffering.

In these terms we can recognize in Salinger's novel an example of the initiatory experience that becomes necessary at the end of adolescence. It is not necessarily encountered at that time, nor is it carried through then; but that is the age period at which the tensions and the transformation most naturally occur. If it is not brought to culmination then, the inner confusions and restlessness will continue to exert their pressures on the personality until the initiation into maturity does take place. The intervening period is then bound to be a time of troubles characterized by inadequacies in life, neurotic styles of behavior, and much emotional pain. It is this pain and inner pressure that Salinger enables us to see in the late adolescent pressing toward an initiation experience in the new form that is becoming characteristic of modern times.

Other novelists of the past generation have also described the unconscious strivings toward rebirth in the modern adolescent. Most notable of these among European authors is Hermann Hesse, especially in his short, autobiographical

---

*Ibid., p. 202

novel, *Demian*. It is probably correct to say that the entire corpus of Hesse's work constitutes a source of evidence and documentation for our basic conception that personality growth takes place through successive depths of initiation at the various stages of life. In Hesse as in Salinger, we see an illustration of the fact that the initiation of personality to its next level of development at the adolescent stage takes place, not ritually as at earlier periods of culture, but through a lonely inner struggle.

Underlying this struggle is the pressing need to make a connection with reality in ultimate terms. It is a need so overwhelming that it often precipitates situations that force the individual to the razor's edge in a struggle whose goal is the opening of a new perception of meaning in life. We could see in the experience of Franny, as would also be the case with Demian and others, that this struggle bears the main characteristics of initiatory experiences.

It does indeed lead to an initiation into life in terms of a new realization, but the characteristic of the modern experience is that it takes place without the support and without the protection of any socially instituted ritual. The modern individual has to go it alone. His initiation comes about in a totally unstructured way, the crisis and the resolution being brought about altogether unexpectedly and with no preparation. It is given no format by the culture, and yet it spontaneously follows the patterns that are found in the ceremonials of initiation in primitive cultures and in the history of religion. This is an indication of a necessary development that is inherent in the growth process of the psyche, and which therefore expresses itself in individuals' lives regardless of the culture in which they live.

The initiation to life takes place in modern times in psychological terms and with characteristics that are indicative of the present crises in culture. It is an experience through which the individual passes alone without the support of social ceremonials since the symbols which once lay behind the rituals are no longer meaningful to him. His experience therefore has no directive pattern, but only a spontaneous one brought about through the apparent happenstance of life. But, because of this, each initiation to life in the modern world has the quality of a unique personal destiny. Being less structured, it is less protected; and being more individual, it is more lonely as well as more painful. It occurs in the midst of one's existence in the world, and it draws its contents not from ancient myths but from the actual events of its daily life. It may eventually touch the depths of ultimate reality with this, thus transmuting its actual existence into the dimension of the mythologic, but that is both the pain and the possibility of the modern initiatory experience.

At this point in our discussion, we must indicate some additional considerations concerning the role of initiation in psychological growth. These warrant much fuller treatment than we can give them here, but they must at least be outlined in order that the perspective of our remarks can be clearer.

We have already made the general anthropological observation that in the majority of cultures the most appropriate time for initiation to take place is at the time of late adolescence. In some societies the chronological age at which this occurs is earlier than in others, and the tendency in modern civilization is for it to be significantly later. Of much greater consequence, however, than the specific age at which it occurs is the fact that the first initiation to take place in an individual's life tends to become the prototype for all the initiations that will follow through the later stages of development.

More is involved in this than the experience of initiation itself. The first basic initiation through which the individual passes, whether ritually or spontaneously and personally, opens the pathway and becomes the model for all subse-

quent movements in the personality, for future transformations in point of view, and further enlargements in the
capacities of awareness and activity.

Each unit of time in an individual's life is ruled by a governing symbol. Symbols that are large enough to have this
governing capacity tend also to have an ultimate and elemental quality in whose terms individuals can have experiences
of connection*. Each *governing symbol* also carries an image
of reality that applies to its period of history. Each significant
psychological time-unit is thus based upon a particular vision of reality. What is of special importance, however, is not
the content of this vision but the quality of inner seeing with
which it is perceived. This involves the subjective experience
of a vision of reality in which transpersonal symbols are involved. At stake is the individual's recognition of the nature
of his personal identity in relation to the particular view of
life that his society and his psyche have made available to
him. There are inevitably several levels at which such large
symbols can be perceived, and this is why the crucial factor is
not the symbol itself but the quality of intensity with which it
is experienced. Since the images that are capable of serving
as governing symbols are necessarily vast in their depth and
scope, everything depends on the way one gains access to
them, how they are entered, and how fully one becomes capable of participating in them. An aspect of this is shown in
the fact that ceremonials of initiation are frequently spoken
of as *rites d'entrée*. They are designed as means of *entering*
larger dimensions of symbolism, which means larger visions
of reality, than had been accessible to the individual before.
This is indeed the essence of an initiation experience.

The point of such experiences is that, by means of them,
the individual receives an awareness of personal identity not

*Progroff, Ira, *The Practice of Process Meditation*, Dialogue House Library, New
York, 1980, Part III, Chapter 9-12.

merely in terms of subjective feelings nor of his immediate, sensually perceived world, but in the context of transpersonal symbols. That is why the religious quality of initiation is so important throughout the history of culture. In each culture the particular religion is the carrier of the myths and through its ceremonials it gives the individual a personally effective introduction to the mythological gods and heros. In that way it provides a means of direct contact by which the elemental symbols of life may be entered.

In situations like those that we encounter characteristically in modern times, situations in which there is neither a traditional ritual nor an established symbol placed at the individual's disposal, transpersonal and mythological symbols are just as fully involved in the experience of reality. The only difference is that instead of being entered ritually, they are entered under the pressure of the inward struggles of personality, the strivings and frustrations, the disturbances, dreams, and visions, which comprise the inner content of personal existence in modern life. The modern individual is brought to his experience of reality in terms of symbols that are transpersonal in scope, but they are opened to him by means of the intimate events of his inner life. Since the modern person is forced as an isolated individual into depth encounters that would in other cultures be buffered for him by social rituals, we can readily understand that the first experience in which this takes place is of critical importance. If it is difficult, prolonged, or unduly painful, it may have traumatic consequences, impeding further development because of the fears and resistances that it engenders. But if this first recognition of personal identity in terms of a larger view of reality is a strong and reassuring experience, it will serve as an excellent model for further personal explorations into the unknown areas of reality, and it will greatly expedite the growth of personality in later years.

For each individual there is, therefore, great importance

in the *prototypal initiation* since future transitions, moving from one time-unit to another in the individual's life, will tend to follow its pattern. The effect of each initiation experience is to bring about a new sense of personal identity in terms of an extended symbolization of reality. Each time this takes place effectively, it establishes a new image of reality for the individual and this defines a new approach to life and a new period of activity in his existence. Each iniatory experience thus sets up a time-unit in the individual's life, a unit that is ruled in each case by a particular governing symbol.

The first of these time-units in a person's existence is established by the prototypal initiation. As long as its governing symbol remains fruitful and meaningful, it retains its position in the psyche. For that long, that unit of time with its image of reality endures. When, however, its meaning wanes so that it no longer functions well, confusions appear within the psyche, and disturbances enact themselves in external behavior. These disturbances are often manifested in the flow of dreams where they express the same, or equivalent, symbolizations of death and rebirth which are observed culturally in the rituals of initiation. In this case, it is the death of the old governing image and the birth of a new one.

The modern person lives through the equivalent of the death and rebirth of initiation, but he does so within his own life in terms of his dreams and other inward symbolic perceptions. This takes place not only in his first *prototypal initiation*, but in the *successive initiations* that are the vehicles for the ongoing movement and continuing growth of the psyche all through the individual's life.

These *successive initiations* correspond to what I have referred to in another context as *hinge experiences*. They are like hinges on a door in that they provide the possibility of passage from one room to another. The successive initiations mark the movement from one time-unit to another for they carry the transition from one governing perception of meaning to the newborn image replacing it.

These successive initiations which are the hinges between the time-units in the individual's life follow the same form and pattern as the prototypal initiations. Their content, however, is progressively new, expressing the unfoldment and the deepening of the person's relationship to life. Viewed retrospectively in terms of their continuity they may be seen as the steppingstones by which the path of the individual's existence is formed.

We must recognize the fact that often an individual considers himself fortunate if he has successfully passed through only a single initiation experience in his entire life. When, on the other hand, a prototypal initiation is followed by successive initiations their effect is to take the individual past the *plateau* of social adjustment of which we spoke earlier and to draw him forward to progressively new unfoldments of the potentials of his life. These are the creative events of personality, and it is out of their continuity that the meaning of human existence emerges in the individual life.

17

The Life Task: Outer Work and Inner Opus

The fourth of the chronological stages in our listing is that of early maturity, approximately the years from twenty to thirty. This is the time when the individual discovers his special life task and when he embarks on the personal involvement that will lead in the direction of fulfilling it. Naturally, this stage will begin at a younger age in those cultures where initiation comes earlier; and it may begin quite a bit later in cultural situations like those of modern times.

Essentially there are two life-needs which the initiation experience must eventually meet. The first of these is that the individual achieve a recognition of personal identity in the context of a transpersonal and inherently symbolic view of the universe. The second is that this general perception be such that it translates itself for the individual into a specific path of activity that will indicate the particular form and content of the life. In the initiations of primitive tribes both of these needs are often filled in a single initiation. When the boy is separated from the women's group and is taken through the ceremony from which he is to emerge as a man, he also is given a field of work, as hunter or fisherman, or whatever the tribe's economy and traditions require. Similarly when the girl is cermonially inducted into womanhood, she is given a place in the tribe's view of reality, and the pattern of her life activity is laid out for her.

In more developed cultures, however, this dual function tends to be broken into its separate parts. Thus in western culture, especially in earlier generations when its symbols were still effective, there was first the religious ceremonial of initiation into a spiritual universe, as in the Christian Confirmation ceremony or in the Hebraic Bar Mitzvah, and later the induction to a field of work through acceptance into a craft guild after a period of apprenticeship. This latter phase went together with the earning of a livelihood, marriage, and the establishment of a household. Thus the two aspects of initiation, taken together, provided the main components necessary for a mature life in the community, and they set the individual on the pathway of his own existence.

In the chronological outline we are working with, the first of these initiations, the initiation into a context of meaning, takes place in the third period, the period of later adolescence. The second initiation, the initiation into a life-work, takes place characteristically in the fourth period between the ages of twenty and thirty. This is the time, we must note, when the central dialectic process of the psyche begins to take effect. It is in this aspect of the process, in fact, that the encompassing dialectic of the psyche is enabled to fulfill itself.

We recognize that in these successive initiations an overarching process of personal development is involved. Where cultural symbols are effective, the initiation rituals enact the stages of the process with the support of a social context. The characteristic of the modern situation, however, is that the contemporary individual experiences the process of personal growth in terms, not of rituals, but of the direct psychological content of the process itself, in terms of dreams, desires, anxieties, and other intimate events.

A good illustration of the psychological process involved

in the modern person's initiation is the following dream of a young woman in her early twenties. Both in cultural background and in education, the dreamer is similar to Salinger's Franny of whom we have spoken. She had however come one step further in the inner process of her initiation to life, for she was at the point where a decision was being made concerning her life-work to determine whether she would continue as a teacher of small children or would embark on something new. It was at that point of decision that she had this dream.

There were many women present of all kinds and styles. There was also an old woman there, a witchlike woman, and the feeling in the dream was that this old woman was the possessor both of great wisdom and of social authority. She was the one who could say what should be done, and she was also the one to carry it out.

The situation in the dream was that all the varied women who were standing grouped together were to be killed, and that this was to be done by the old woman. She was in fact engaged in slowly and methodically stoning each of the women to death.

At first, the feeling in the dream was that this would be a ghastly thing to observe, and that it would be a horrible experience. At first, the dreamer was disturbed about how painful it would be for each of the women being killed in this way. As the dream proceeded, however, it turned out that the stonings were not actually painful. The women simply died when the old woman stoned them. They died gracefully and painlessly without protest. They seemed to accept the fact of the stonings as a necessary event, and even as something that was good and beneficial.

There then came into the dream picture another woman who stood at the edge of the group of women who were to be killed. This woman was young and very beautiful, and there was an aura about her that indicated that she was in some way a special person. She was holding an infant in her arms, and she was also part of the group of women who were waiting their turn to be stoned. The indication was that she also would be killed when her turn came. Soon, however, it became clear that the old witch woman had a special interest in this beautiful woman, and that her life would be spared together with that of her child.

The old woman slowly and methodically continued her project of stoning the women to death. One by one, she carried out her task and at length the work was finished. Now the atmosphere of the dream was placid and satisfying, as though a good and necessary work had been well done. The bodies had to be disposed of, but there was the feeling that this would be taken care of in some proper and orderly way without any difficulty or inconvenience.

At this point, there was an abrupt change in the scene. The bodies of the stoned women were now gone and the dreamer found herself in a picnic atmosphere seated on a large and very pleasant lawn or meadow. Together with her were the old witch woman, the young, beautiful woman whose life had been spared, and also her baby. The old witch woman was now in a warm, happy, and expansive mood. She and the dreamer were playing with the baby on the grass while a picnic lunch was being made ready for all of them to eat. The feeling tone as the dream ended was warm and joyous and promising.

The initiation aspect of such a dream is indeed obvious. A death is required in order that the next step in life may take place. It is undoubtedly for this reason that the deaths are not represented as being unpleasant in the dream. They have a constructive function in that they clear away the past. When the question was placed before the dreamer of who was actually killed in the dream, it seemed clear to her that the women who were stoned were an aggregation representing all of the varieties of womanhood that one finds in society. These were all the external selves that she might be, but the sense of the dream was that they were all to be eliminated. They were to be killed and buried, and the old witch woman, whose aspect was that of uncanny wisdom, was the one who would bring it about. Only a single person in the dream was not to die, and that was the image of the dreamer as idealized potentiality, the young and beautiful woman she might be. This was the part of herself that was the bearer of a newly born child, an emergent new being which held the promise of her future self. The dream thus followed the initiation pattern in dramatizing the rejection and death of the various social types of womanhood, and in indicating a rebirth, or new birth, in a being that would draw its sources from the inner self.

The central dialectic of the process of psychological growth is expressed in this. While the essence of this process is that it proceeds according to the analogy of a plant growing out of its seed, the fact of the social nature of man brings it about that the personality is formed in continuous interrelationship with the environment. By an unconscious osmosis and an involuntary mimicry, the individual develops patterns of behavior, attitudes, and even images of the self that are drawn from outside himself and not from the seed within. These are *derivative images* rather than *seed images*. They reflect the lives of other people in the individual's social environment, rather than the individual himself. They are not integrally connected with the roots of the individual's own personality, and to this degree one cannot expect that authentic growth will come forth from them. It is psychologically necessary then that these derivative images be eliminated, killed off, before authentic growth can begin. This is the dialectical process which the initiation ritual, as typified in the dream, carries through.

Now, in this fourth chronological period of life development, we come to the second aspect of initiation that is essential for the maturation of the individual. The effect of the first phase was to reach past the derivative images to make contact with one's own identity. But now, in the second phase, it is necessary that the images that arise within the individual find their appropriate expression, and their appropriate *form*, in the outer world. The process of growth moves forward in time, and it moves outward in direction. But this is in order that the image that is behind the growth process in the individual may fulfill itself inwardly.

The initiation experience in which one makes contact with one's own identity is the true beginning of the individual's existence. It is then that it begins to be possible for him to discover what course his life is to take and what is to be required of him. In this sense we may speak of a *life task* that is unique for each individual in so far as it is inherent in the seed of his being and in the embodiment of his personal destiny.

The roots or causes of this can certainly not be named definitively. All we can say of it is that the image that carries the personal destiny of the individual contains everything that is present as a potentiality within him. It includes his biological nature. It includes the social factors that are part of his individuality. And it includes the historical components of personality in all their elusive aspects, even including those elements of personal destiny whose source must be sought before or beyond the individual's birth. All these belong to the specific image of individuality, the *dynatype*, which unfolds in the individual's existence and sets the requirements of the individual life.

The life task is both inward and outward. It is inward in so far as its core is an image of potentiality that moves out of the depth of personality. It is outward in the sense that it can unfold and fulfill itself only as it engages in activities in the world. It is by means of this two-fold nature that the dialectic of the psyche is expressed in the unfoldment of the life task. The process of growth begins with an image that is felt or perceived intuitively within the psyche. Its nature requires it to be projected outward and placed upon another person, or upon a tangible work to be done. As it carries out the work, or as it lives out the relationship, the image, which had been only a potentiality before, becomes real. It takes on form, and thus it becomes actual.

At this point the artwork becomes an entity existent in its own right. It had begun as an image within the individual, but as it is concretized and begins to be formed, it acquires its own individuality. It has its own inherent needs which derive from the process by which form is given to it. For example, when a man conceives in the depth of his psyche an idea for a novel, his first step in making it an actuality is to give it form. He begins to work on it by outlining the direction it is to take and by starting the work of shaping it. At this point it is his artwork. It is altogether *his* for it is totally derived from his inner image.

Once he has begun to give it form, however, the image that was within him is now also in the artwork. Once it has been embodied in the outer work, the image is subject to an altogether new and additional dimension of pressures and needs. It must satisfy the requirements of form now, not any longer in terms of the subjectivity of the image, but in terms of objective standards. It is as though the novel had a consciousness of its own and were aware of the fact that it must meet the criteria not only of the person who originated it but of others who will read it. More important still, it is as though the novel were aware that it possesses an inner principal, an image of its own potential meaning, and that this needs to be fulfilled with integrity. The embryonic novel then sets forth its own requirements of form, and at that point it is as though a dialogue were set in motion between the artwork and its author. The novel declares its needs. If the author can hear and respond to what the novel is saying to him, a continuing dialogue will be established in which the author and his work will interact upon each other, each influencing and enlarging the other's capacities, each bringing to fulfill-ment more of the image of potentiality that is latent in the other.

We are all familiar in the history of art and literature with works in which it is quite obvious that the author did not permit himself to conduct a dialogue with his work-in-progress. In many novels, poems, plays and paintings one feels that the author deliberately and even willfully foisted his original conception onto his artwork, and then insisted upon it so that the artwork was forced to fit into a precon-ceived mold. Only a monologue took place then in the act of creation, and thus the artwork was not free to draw forth the integrity of its own natural form. The reader or viewer of such an artwork cannot avoid the feeling that the work has had something external superimposed upon it, so that it seems artificially constructed.

On the other hand, the result is quite different when an author is able to listen to his artwork and to engage in a genuine dialogue with it as with a person. Then the work-in-progress, which the author originated by projecting his own image outward into the work, becomes like a child that is growing toward adolescence and is bringing forth its own integral nature. Listening to it as it speaks to him, the author can learn how its inner image needs to unfold in order to express itself most effectively. Permitting it to have its effect upon him in relation to his own image in the depths of his psyche, he can then respond to its need in terms of his own. This is dialogue. He can then be flexible enough and sensitive enough to enable his artwork to reach a *form* which is proper and authentic and integral with itself. As he does this in di-alogue, the image unfolding in himself, which brought the artwork into existence in the first place, is also enabled to reach the integral form that is authentic for it. Thus, the more openly and unreservedly the artwork is enabled to fulfill its inner need in form, the more its author is enabled to achieve the unique and authentic form of himself as a person. We may speak then of *the principle of the mutuality of form* as a key to the process of creativity. For this is how creativity happens, as the two meet. The artist and his artwork draw forth each other, each evoking the essence of the other, until the outer form expresses the inner image of each, the person and the artwork.

In the context of what has been said, it must be clear that when we use the term *artwork* we are not referring necessarily to a project carried out in the field of the fine arts. The artwork may be undertaken in a medium of the arts, as a novel or a poem or a painting; but it will equally be an artwork in our psychological sense if it is a business venture or an undertaking in politics. The identifying characteristic that defines it as an artwork is that it is an outer embodiment of the inner image by which the process of personal growth and the fulfillment of the life task is carried through. It involves projection, a throwing forth, of the inner image so that it can take an outer form, and in that form talk back to the person in a dialectical dialogue. By means of this dialogue with its dialectical movement to and fro, the inner form of personality is drawn to greater unity and crystallization. In this development it parallels the gradual and craftsmanlike crystallization of an authentic outer form for the artwork.

The principle of the mutuality of form holds a key to the dialectic of creativity, and to the process of personal growth as well. As the seed of individuality unfolds in each human being, each reaching toward its unique personal destiny, a life task gradually discloses itself. It is seldom possible to predict what this will be; for there is the great danger that one will be controlling and thereby manipulating one's future in terms of the habits of the past. It does, however, steadily reveal itself in the course of a life to those who learn how to look for it and are patient enough to wait. It shows itself in subjective intimations of the future and also it may be observed in the patterned coincidences of time occurring in one's life. One or two or three successfully completed artworks seen in retrospect may serve as markers that indicate the road on which one is heading. But generally one knows only after the fact, and very seldom before. The inner perception of one's life is a feeling of a movement into the future, an unfolding. The content of this movement cannot be perceived truly, however, while it remains on the inside. It is still only a potentiality while it is there. It only becomes clearly visible when it is embodied in an outer form and has been expressed in an external work. This is the great task: to make the outer form of the artwork adequate and appropriate to the two images that lie behind it, the image in the artwork and the image in the person himself.

The perfection of the form of the artwork is an *outer work*, but it corresponds to an *inner work*. In the continuing dialogue between outer and inner, each significant step in the perfection of the form of the artwork contributes a psy-chic increment which accumulates bit by bit in the depths of personality. Each artwork in the course of a life makes an additional deposit as it is brought to its appropriate form. Slowly it builds in size and solidity in a way that is very similar to the formation of the oyster's pearl, the symbolic "pearl of great cost". The pearl is formed through the frictions and tensions involved in struggling to bring the *outer works* of one's life task successfully to their proper form. And in the course of this, gradually and cumulatively, an *inner opus* is formed at the core of personality representing the cumulative achievement of *form* in *outer works*. This *opus* is the *inner form* of the person.

Now the principle of the mutuality of form has taken the creative process of life one step further. On the outer level it has brought an artwork to culmination, drawing forth its possibilities and giving them expression in an integral and aesthetic form. On the inner level, it has carried to realization an image that was present in the person as a potentiality. Thus a new form has been created within the person corresponding to the new form that has been created in the artwork. The mutuality of this process is indeed a spiritual event. By means of it, the dialectic of the psyche fulfills itself and leads to a new synthesis. The opposites of inner and outer, of subject and object, are brought into a reciprocal relationship, and the establishment of this unity of form where only shapeless potentiality has been before is a creative event that extends the process of life.

Once it has happened, and in each individual situation in which is has happened, it is a creative event that extends the life of the spirit in the human species. The reciprocal fulfillment of the inner image and the outer work brings an increment of spiritual meaning to the life of the person. It is indeed in this way that meaning unfolds in an individual's life; for meaning is composed of the increments of creative events by which opposites are transformed as new entities. The continuity of this is the life of the spirit, and is the process by which the inner opus of individuality is progressively enlarged.

Events of this kind have a creative and spiritual meaning not only for the individual who is involved in them, but for mankind as a whole. Each new increment to the opus of selfhood is an addition to the permanent heritage of civilization. These creative events, by which new experiences of unity emerge from the principle of the mutuality of form, are the individual bricks with which the spiritual history of mankind is built.

In the process by which new artworks are created, the main factor is the primary image by which the work is conceived and originated. Inevitably the final form of the artwork will bear something of the stamp of this, as it will also of necessity reflect the quality of craftsmanship with which the outer work was carried through. In addition to these aspects, however, wherever the forming of an outer artwork has resulted in increments to the inner opus, the tone of the opus will be reflected in the artwork as well. In such cases the artwork has a quality that reaches far beyond the merely artistic success of its aesthetic form. It carries an overlay of spirit which shines through and around the artwork and makes it a lasting point of contact for individuals in generations to come. Such an artwork serves as an awakener of meaning for many, and in the course of time becomes a lastingly effective symbol for the community at large. It can serve as such a symbol because it retains the quality of tension and of depth in the midst of which it was made. This quality is capable of speaking to many persons in all parts of history, for it recreates the dialogue out of which an outer work and an inner opus are mutually formed.

This is the essence of the great masterpieces that have been created through the ages. They reach out beyond themselves because the quality of the dialogue out of which they were formed lives on in their atmosphere long after the act of creation has been consummated. This atmosphere awakens in others the fulness of what the mutuality of the creative act involved when it was taking place. And by means of it many others can experience the liberating unity in a creative event on the level and in the context of their own lives.

The individuals by whom the great artworks of history have been brought forth are persons who leapt off the plateau of culture to make a creative act of their moment in time. Taken together, their works constitute humanity's collective leap beyond the confines of earthly life, the cumulative building of an opus that is progressively the spiritual history of mankind's future. It is thus that the reality of spirit establishes itself, building itself out of the accretion of personal experiences that form the transpersonal dimension of human existence.

PART THREE

In the

Twilight Range

18

Waking Dreams and Living Myth: The Process of Creativity in Ingmar Bergman

The subject of dream and myth reaches to the core of the nature of man. On the one hand, dreams and especially myths are a primary medium for intuitive insights into the ultimate nature of human existence. On the other hand, the conception that each culture has of myths and dreams reflects its underlying view of the nature of man. For modern man, this conception has changed significantly during the past two centuries. Where myths and dreams were once seen as religious realities, they were later narrowed down by rationalism. More recently, however, their larger significance has been restored to them in a context broader than rationalism; but now, in our era of highly developed intellect, they are seen mainly as a means of gaining access to ancient intuitive insights into the nature of human existence.*

Because of this new recognition, it is particularly important to have an adequate perspective regarding the place and role of dream and myth in the context of total human personality. To this end, I shall undertake to set before you in the

---

*This paper was originally given as an address to the *Society for the Arts, Religion and Contemporary Culture.* It was published in Joseph Campbell, editor, *Myths, Dreams, and Religion*, Dutton, New York, 1970.

following pages some of the chief aspects of myth and dream as seen in the light of holistic depth psychology. I think you will find that these perspectives are useful not only for understanding the factors that underlie the nature of symbolism in ancient and modern times, but also for actively evoking the potentials of personality at deep levels of symbolic experience.

You will notice in the title of this paper the phrase, "waking dreams." The word "waking" used there is intended not so much to indicate a contrast with dreams of sleep as to convey the largeness of the dream dimension. Dreams are not restricted to the physical condition of sleep. They pertain rather to the symbolic dimension of human experience as a whole. Thus, dreams may occur in sleep where we are accustomed to look for them; in waking states where we find ourselves living out the symbolic aspect of life; and in twilight states that are between the state of sleeping and waking.

Dreaming in all three of these conditions expresses an underlying quality, not only of human existence but of the nature of the human psyche. This is specifically the quality of the psyche that unfolds in terms of symbols. It may come in the form either of symbolic imagery, symbolic experiences or the intuitive perceptions of the symbolic meaning of life. It may be any of these, for all of these together constitute the symbolic dimension of human experience.

In general, dreams are the aspect of the symbolic dimension that is experienced in personal terms. When the symbolic dimension is perceived in transpersonal terms, in terms that pertain to more than the subjective experience of the individual but reach to what is universal in man, whether the experience is in sleeping or waking, myth is involved. It is myth because it touches what is ultimate as the truths of existence in human life, because it expresses profound elusive truths symbolically, and because it provides an inner perspective by which the transpersonal mysteries of human existence can be felt intimately and entered into personally.

In this sense it is quite clear that there are often mythological aspects of dreams. When a personal experience is felt deeply enough, it touches what is more than personal in man's existence. The process of dreaming therefore moves naturally from the personal level to the level of myth. This is how it becomes possible for individuals to experience their personal lives in larger-than-personal contexts of meaning.

Both dream and myth are aspects of a single dimension of experience, the symbolic dimension. To think of dreams in terms of this dimension is separate from, though not necessarily contradictory to, other lines of investigation. For example, considerable advances have recently been made in the physiological understanding of dreams. Experiments have been conducted into the various conditions under which dreams have been produced. Through them, considerable information has been gathered concerning the biological and neurological aspects of dreaming in the sleep state. Such investigations have helped us understand that sleep dreams are a physiological necessity for the nervous system. The evidence accumulated indicates that dreams are an integral part of the life process of the human organism.

It must be pointed out, however, that such psychological studies treat dreams specifically in their sleep aspect. While they provide valuable information for understanding the physiological base of dreaming, they do not directly contribute to the understanding of dreams as expressions of the symbolic dimension of human experience. In one sense it would be correct to say that these sleep studies of dreams, dealing as they do with the physiological conditions, are *quantitative* whereas studies of dreams in terms of their symbolic components are *qualitative.* The physiological study of dreaming makes observations about the tangible, outer side of it, while the qualitative study of dreams and myths deals with the intangible aspects of human existence. It deals with the symbolic forms by which human beings reach toward personal meaning in their individual lives, and reach toward a larger, transpersonal meaning via the fundamental and elusive truths of human existence. This qualitative and essentially intangible symbolic aspect of dreams and myths is the special province and interest of holistic depth psychology. It undertakes to help individuals find the direction and meaning of their lives, drawing in large part on the guidance that is given by dreams and other nonconscious expressions of the person's interior life.

Another aspect of the study of dreams that has been historically important and is still applied in many varieties of psychotherapy is the interpretation of dreams as expressions of unconscious processes. The hypothesis of the unconscious is indeed the historical basis for the development of depth psychology as a special discipline. A great deal depends, however, on the way in which this aspect of the psyche is conceived.

In the first place, as Sigmund Freud described the unconscious, it was specifically related to the repressed contents of personality. With respect to dreams, Freud's view was essentially that dreams are the carriers of the repressed contents of the psyche. He held that dreams refer symbolically to those past experiences that the individual is unable to accept by the light of his conscious attitudes. Implicitly, in such a context, symbols are not regarded as an integral form of human experience but as secondary and derivative. In Freud's framework, symbols are substitutes for the original experiences, which had to be repressed because they could not be consciously faced.

This conception of dreams and their contents possesses an inherent limitation that has become increasingly apparent during the past decade of psychotherapeutic work. As

secretary to the psychoanalytic movement during its beginnings, Otto Rank is undoubtedly the man who saw this
limitation first and called attention to it. The man who responded to it most constructively, however, was C. G. Jung.
Jung accepted and retained Freud's hypothesis of the unconscious, but he saw the necessity of broadening it. In re-
formulating Freud's original conception, Jung made a
contribution of tremendous historical importance, the implications of which are only now beginning to be appreciated. I
doubt that in time to come it will be possible for any psychological orientation to achieve a real insight into myth and
dream without assimilating the meaning of Jung's reformulation of Freud.

In his new view, which he formulated around the time of
World War I, Jung divided the unconscious into two levels.
The first, the surface level, he called the Personal Unconscious. It was in most regards the same as Freud's conception
of the Unconscious Repressed. He then described a deeper
level which he called the Collective Unconscious. To this area
of the psyche Jung ascribed those dreams and patterns of
symbolism that have a transpersonal quality. Jung's use of
the word *collective* here must be understood more in its Ger-
man than in its English sense. He meant *kollectiv*, which has
the overtone not so much of the multiple experience of the
group as of the inherently human. This deeper level, then,
the Collective Unconscious, must be understood as contain-
ing those patterns of symbolism that occur in the psyches of
individuals, not because of their individuality and not because they are members of particular groups, but because
they are human beings. These are patterns of symbolism that
pertain to mankind as a whole, or, in Jung's language, the
archetypes.

Jung's addition to Freud's basic hypothesis significantly
enlarged the possibilities of appreciating symbols by the light
of depth psychology. It did, however, retain the basic dicho-

tomy between consciousness as the surface of the psyche and the unconscious with its various levels of depth. Experience in psychotherapy subsequent to Jung's reformulation has increasingly indicated that this division is artificial and restrictive. Although it is of the greatest importance to maintain the conception of depth in man, the distinction between consciousness and the unconscious seems not any longer to be tenable. We require a unitary way of conceiving the psyche, so that we will have an open and flexible way of representing the continuous movement that takes place within it.

The working model of man that is used by holistic depth psychology is that of the *Organic Psyche.** In this conception, the psychological nature of man is regarded as an organic unity in which a continuous process expressing the cycles of growth and decay takes place. This process is comparable to and contains all the essential qualities of the process of growth that is found in the world of nature. The functioning of the Organic Psyche, therefore, may best be understood in terms of a metaphor of the seed, which is an image that appears in the mythologies and philosophies of many peoples.

The process of growth out of the seed is a movement that is determined not by the past experiences of the individual but by the teleological goal that is inherent in each species. The seed carries the potentialities of development for each species, and therefore for each individual. In this sense, by analogy, the processes of the Organic Psyche are the carriers of the growth possibilities of each individual member of the species. To the extent, then, that we would retain the use of the original term, the unconscious, the time aspect of that concept is essentially reversed. Instead of the unconscious as Freud originally thought of it expressing the past experiences

---

*See Ira Progoff, *Depth Psychology and Modern Man*, 1959, McGraw Hill, New York.

which the individual had to repress, the unconscious now becomes the container and the carrier of those experiences that have not yet happened. The unconscious, as the seed aspect of the personality, contains the possibilities for future experience. It is unconscious because it has specifically not yet been lived.

Because of the perspective in which it sets human life in relation to time—essentially reversing the roles of past and future—this unitary reformulation of the nature of the psyche, and specifically of the unconscious, is of the greatest importance for understanding the psychological process that is involved in dreams. A great many dreams, of course, are expressions of past experiences and also of repressed experiences. A much more significant part, however, if not quantitatively then formatively and qualitatively, are expressions of experiences that are seeking to become real in the future.

There is much more than the sleep aspect of dreams involved in this. For example, in the popular use of the word "dreamer" there is an overtone that is quite additional to the meaning of "dreamer" as one who is asleep. A person is referred to as a "dreamer" when people regard him as having a visionary quality. He is a dreamer because his attention goes away from a narrow focus on the past or even on the specific present, but moves into visionary perceptions of the future. He is a dreamer, therefore, not because he is asleep but because, in his waking state, his attention is turned symbolically to the possibilities of the future. He is a dreamer because he has intimations of what may become true of his life in future time. This expresses the important quality of dreams as a symbolic movement in waking life as well as in sleeping life toward the possibilities of the future in the light of new and larger contexts of meaning.

In working with the organic conception of the psyche we are using a perspective that sees the human being as a part of the world of nature. The processes of the psyche follow the same patterns of growth as those that are found throughout the natural world. This is true, but only up to a certain point. At the point where the human species takes a step forward in its development and goes beyond the level that the evolutionary process had reached when man emerged, an additional factor is added. This factor is the inherent dialectic of the human psyche. It is a movement of opposites that is expressed throughout the life process of human beings. It is movement from inner to outer.

In this conception, the growth process of individual personality proceeds as a movement from inner to outer, beginning with the seed of possibility at the depths of the psyche. The potentials of individuality are present as drives toward particular types of activity. These activities carry the energies that are latent at the seed level of the psyche. They are expressed as images, and also as symbolic patterns both of visions and of acts of behavior. They start on the inner level, on the dream level of personality, and they move outward, taking the form of outer works. They become the outer expressions that correspond to the inner drive toward growth in the form of life activities.

As these works are carried through and completed, the inner drives, which are the patterns of potential behavior inherent at the organic seed level of each personality, are brought to fulfillment. As the image is actualized in a work, content is given to the personality. It is thus that a sense of unique personal meaning, an inner myth of personality, builds in the individual and gives him an actively inner way of relating to the world around him.

It is important to realize that these outer works are equally as symbolic as the contents of sleep dreams. This is so primarily because their source is to be found in the images at the deeper than conscious levels of personality. Outer works thus become part of that larger category of life activities that are the enactment of inner images in the midst of waking life. These are the *in vivo* dreams, the dreams that are lived in the aliveness of our social existence. They are the outer correspondents of the inner process by which the non-conscious potentials of the Organic Psyche are lived and enacted in the outer world.

Probably the most succinct way to illustrate the fullness of the process involved here is by referring to the lives and works of creative persons. The phrase "creative person" has perhaps been used much too loosely in recent years, but in the context of our discussion there are some objective criteria by which such a category of persons can be discerned and the characteristic nature of their life experiences described. Essentially, these are persons in whom the creative process of the psyche has been allowed to happen, and who have also been able to draw the dialectic of the psyche forward in their life experience. Their creativity consists essentially in their ability to move freely from the inner level to the outer level, and continue to go back and forth. The creative person is one who is able to draw upon the images within himself and then to embody them in outer works, moving inward again and again for the inspiration of new source material, and outward again and again to learn from his artwork what it wants to become while he is working on it.

In speaking of the creative person in these terms no judgment is implicitly being made, neither about the quality of the creative works nor about the person, nor about the authenticity with which the creative person is engaged in the dialectical process of the psyche. He may have contact with the deep level of images in himself because he is a profoundly centered person, or he may have this contact because he is so disturbed and split that the inner imagery is fragmented and forces itself upon him. At the other pole, the creative person may have contact with his outer work for equally opposing reasons. It may be because he has experienced a transpersonal commitment to uniting the inner and outer worlds within his life, or it may be because he is in the grip of a compulsion to keep working at something.

There is a full range of degrees within these opposites, and the quality of the artwork will surely reflect the place on the scale at which the work has been done. Whatever the reasons that a person embarks on the continuous communication between the inner and outer worlds, whether because of a compulsion or because of a calling, it seems that if he remains committed to the dialectical process something new and unexpected emerges in his life. It is as though the core of a center forms within him. A new self forms, not from his directly seeking it, but as a side effect of the integrity with which he continues his inner-outer journey. With this new self there also comes a capacity of consciousness, a quality of realization, that adds a major dimension to his life. This awareness also could not be achieved by directly seeking it; but it comes about indirectly through the integrity of dialectical involvement.

To illustrate this process briefly let me refer to the life and work of Ingmar Bergman. Let me say first that the relation of Bergman's work to the psychological process we are speaking of is not something I discovered myself. One morning when I came to my class on "Creative Persons" at Drew University, the students were excitedly discussing a television broadcast. It seemed that Ingmar Bergman had been interviewed by Lewis Freedman on WNDT-TV in New York City. In response to the questioning, Bergmann had described the intimate feelings with which he approached the making of his films and the way he experienced them in terms of his life as a whole. The reason for the excitement in the class was that the students felt that Bergman had intuitively recognized the principles of depth psychology and was applying them in his work. To verify that, I wrote to the television station for a transcript of the broadcast, and it was graciously sent to me.

It is this unedited transcript of a spontaneous interview program that is the basis for the following commentary.*

The statement by Bergman that awakened my class to the relevance of his work for depth psychology came early in the broadcast. In answer to a question by Lewis Freedman, Bergman was describing the inner criteria by which he knew when he had succeeded in making a film as an artwork. Then he said, "I have understood later, I think about a year ago, that *all my pictures are dreams.* Not in the meaning that I have dreamt them now, but in a way I have—I have written them, and I have seen them before I have written them."

> Everything I have seen or heard inside . . . or felt . . . and then I have used reality. And I have combined reality so exactly as the dreams combine.
>
> And every picture—every one of my pictures are dreams.
>
> And when—and if the audience secretly perhaps have seen inside, suddenly meet in their minds, meet my dreams. And feel that they are close to their dreams. I think that is the best communication. (p. 8)

It seems clear that Bergman has intuitively developed a working conception of dreams that moves fluidly into his art. He has perceived that dreams are not merely imagery experiences that occur in the condition of sleep, but that they include everything that transpires on the symbolic dimension of the psyche. Thus they may occur when the person is actually asleep; they may occur in the twilight state between sleeping and waking; and they may occur in the full waking state when one is actively at work in the midst of the environ-

---

*Radio TV Reports, Inc., Public Broadcast Laboratory, WNDT-TV, New York City.

ment. The quality that defines them as dreams is that they are expressions of the symbolic dimension, which is the source of the material from which artworks are made.

Bergman's films begin with an image that is drawn from the dream level of the psyche. The image is the basic ingredient, but it is only the starting point for the process of creation. It comes from the inner world, and then is taken outward to be mixed with the actualities of life. Out of this intermingling there comes a new reality, a motion picture. Each film that Bergman makes is a combination of his inner and outer worlds to form an artwork that then becomes a new reality, a reality with a life of its own. Each is a *waking dream* of his that gives form to his inner experience and that carries his inner life foreward while it itself is being born.

In the process of being filmed, the waking dream is drawn onward beyond the original vision with which it began. It becomes its own reality, and yet it retains the quality of the dream from which it came. If this creative work is well accomplished so that an authentic artwork is produced, there will be in it not only the flavor of the original dream, but the meaning toward which the dream was reaching.

By carrying the waking dream into the form of an artwork the dream will be extended, and at least in part it will be fulfilled. As it does this, the artwork maintains the psychic atmosphere of the dream dimension. Those members of the audience who are sensitive to this dimension of experience are thus able to enter into it and participate in the dream atmosphere. To this degree, the film which began as Bergman's dream becomes fleetingly the dream of the audience. And in that moment when it has become the audience's dream, it opens access to the entire dream level of the psyche for each receptive person in the audience. Then it is no longer a question of the specific content of particular dreams, but of the encompassing atmosphere of that level of the psyche on which dreams are real. By such an artwork the symbolic dimension of human experience is opened and evoked.

To Bergman this is a main criterion of his success as an artist in the making of films. When through feeling the dream quality of the film, the audience as individuals is brought close to their own dreams, as Bergman says in the interview, this is the best communication. In what sense? Not because something specific has been said, and not because a clear message has been communicated. It is real communication, rather, because the deep level of the psyche has been touched and stirred in persons. This symbolic dimension is an all-pervasive, universal ground of trans-personal meeting in which all persons participate as they become aware of it and as they become sensitive to it. I have worked with this dimension of experience by means of the symbol of the "underground stream" in the series of Entrance Meditations of *The Well and the Cathedral*.*

This deep level of communication is beyond rationality. In the interview, Freedman paraphrases Bergman's sense of the communication that takes place by means of his films. "Like a dream, you don't have to understand it . . . You just have to 'recognize' it."

> The dream is never intellectual. [Bergman adds, extending this thought.] *But when you have dreamt, it can start your intellect. It can start you intellectually. It can give you new thoughts. It can give you a new way of thinking, of feeling. . . . It can give you a new light for your inner landscape. And it can give you suddenly a little bit of a new way of handling your life.* (p. 9)

---

*Ira Progoff, *The Well and the Cathedral*, 1971, Dialogue House Library, New York.

Comments like this are indicative of Bergman's awareness of the capacity for *direct knowing* that is inherent in the
nonrational depths of the psyche. Wisdom is given first by
inward seeing, in visions and images that are *beheld* on the
symbolic dimension. From them inferences may be drawn,
and that is when the derivative steps of intellect can begin. It
is clear from the tone of his conversation with Freedman that
Bergman has had the experience of realizing—whether early
in his life or only in recent years is hard to tell with certainty,
though it is more likely the latter—that dream experiences
are carriers of profound messages for personal and spiritual
understanding. He indicates in the interview that his practice
of extending his dreams in his artworks has had the effect
not only of healing him of persistant problems like his fear of
death, but of guiding him toward a sense of meaning in his
life.

We must note that as an artist Bergman seems to have
found a creative way of working with his personal problems.
It is altogether valid from a point of view of depth psychology. Since Bergman's way is in accord with principles that
underlie the functioning of the psyche, it is not at all surpris-
ing that his private method has had highly productive results.

"I always have been interested in those voices inside you,"
Bergman said in the interview. "I think everybody hears those
voices and those forces." "And I have always wanted to put
them in 'reality,' to put them on the table."

"To put them on the table," means, for Bergman, to accord them the same respect that we give to every other fact of
our life. It means to treat one's inner experiences not as
though they were unreal imaginings but to treat them as
facts, and therefore to relate to them in a serious way. Bergman has apparently done this, at least in recent years and
especially in making certain of his movies like *Through a
Glass Darkly* and *Hour of the Wolf.*

In these films Bergman let the interior factors of his life come out so that they could speak and act. That was the only way he could establish a relationship with them. He let them be free to speak in dialogue and reveal their desires. Only then, too, by expressing their background, their history, their development and also their needs could their negative potency be neutralized. And only then could they communicate their larger message for his life as a whole. Bergman has been able to let this happen, and thus it has been possible for his involvement in his artworks as waking dreams to serve as a means of spontaneous therapy.

Paralelling his open relationship with the inner factors of his life is Bergman's relation to the actors who perform in his films. They serve him not only professionally but also personally.

It has often been noted that the same actors appear in Bergman's films again and again. Partly this is the case because he has the same cast of characters living out their lives in his dreams. Thus the same personality types are called for. But an additional reason is that, since the characters are also figures in his dreams, he needs to feel altogether comfortable and relaxed with them. He needs also to be able to trust them as completely as he can trust his own self, for they are a part of his inner life. Working intimately with the same actors in picture after picture has the effect of building such a relationship of trust and a deeper-than-rational connection.

In working with his actors, once they have been cast and have been given the script to study, Bergman begins by giving them full freedom to speak and to act, quite as though they were figures in his dreams. From what the actors say and do, Bergman draws his inferences as to where his dream-film wants to go and how it can best go there. Thus he is quite explicitly treating his artwork as a waking dream, and in a very profound sense. His films are waking dreams not only in the sense that they often utilize dream experiences that have occurred in a waking state, but because they involve an active working on the dream level as the daily content of Bergman's creative life.

To live this way has the effect of establishing a category of experience beyond the distinctions of sleep dreams and waking dreams. It places the person in the midst of the ongoing unity of life while he is actively working on the symbolic dimension. It brings him actively into the deep ground of experience in such a way that the basic organic process of the psyche can take hold and reestablish its patterns and rhythms of operation. Since the nature of this process is integrative, it tends to draw the entire personality into a progressively centered condition. As this occurs, one result— almost a by-product—is to resolve conflicts that had appeared as personal psychological problems.

In one sense it is not so much that these problems are resolved as that they are dropped off; the development of the personality proceeds beyond them. New *gestalts*, or constellations, of personality are formed, and the old conflicts become irrelevant in the new contexts. As this process of development proceeds, it tends to carry with it new artworks that correspond to the successive gestalts of personality. These new works are creative and are successful as art forms insofar as they become vehicles by which persons other than the creative artist himself are able to reach a dimension of depth in their own experience.

The continuity of such experiences is healing. It is healing because it is a *making whole* of personality through an organic process of inner growth. It is healing both for the creator-dreamer who is the main agent of the process and for the receptive individuals in his audience who participate in the atmosphere that his work establishes.

This healing process is carried by the dialectic of the psyche, which is the hallmark of the creative person. It is the back and forth movement from the inner image to the outer work in a cumulative deepening of involvement. In the course of this organic process new artworks are created and new gestalts of personality are formed. But even beyond these, *something further* is taking place.

This *something further* is what Bergman speaks of as "the holy part of the human being." It is clear that Bergman is not a person who believes in God in any of the traditional terms. He is a *modern man* with all the iconoclastic, idol-breaking overtones that that term implies. Nonetheless, an intimation of spirit emerging and evolving in the background of, in the midst of, and in the interstices of his dreams and artworks is implicit now in whatever Bergman does.

In the interview Lewis Freedman was particularly perceptive with respect to the dimension of spiritual reality present in Bergman's work. He called attention to the symbolic meaning of music in the films, and with his question drew out the core of Bergman's continuing experience.

Music, Bergman says, is for him a symbol of life. And more specifically, it is a symbol of "the small holy part of the human being." (p. 28) But characteristically for Bergman music as a symbol is not merely representational. As a symbol it actively moves and unfolds, opening out ever additional perceptions and experiences of reality.

Music served as such an unfolding symbol in the film *Winter Light.* The original inspiration for that film was the *Symphony of Psalms* by Stravinsky. While listening to it Bergman had a vision come to him. It was a vision of a nineteenth-century man who enters a church alone and goes to the altar where he confronts a picture of Christ and says, "I will stay here until the moment when I see God, when God comes to me."

From this vision Bergman conceived the idea for the film. At that point, he says, "I thought the picture will be about his visions and his illness and his hunger and his waiting for God in this empty church." Gradually, however, the conception altered and grew. It became the vehicle for Bergman to work out within the depths of himself what his attitude could be toward God especially in those times when God does not seem to speak at all, when the sources are dried up.

At the time of making *Winter Light*, Bergman recalls, "I was still convinced that God was somewhere inside the human being. That He had some answer to give us. And the end of the picture was exactly that." Bergman's belief then was simply that man must continue when God does not speak to him. Even when he no longer has belief man must go on with his work and carry out the prescribed religious rituals. He must continue in this way even when there is no holy word to guide him. But one day suddenly God will speak to him. And then what God will say to him is essentially that what he has been doing all along was correct, doing his daily work and performing the religious services, and he should continue doing so for the rest of his days, now fortified by God's assurances. That was the answer Begman gave in *Winter Light*. It was the classic answer of optimistic piety as one finds it in the last paragraphs of Ecclesiastes.

But his struggle with the absence of God continued. The symbol continued to unfold, and it came to further expression in another picture. When he made *The Silence*, Bergman says,

> I was still bleeding after the experience that God didn't exist anymore. But I'm now still convinced that there is no God anymore in the world. That God is dead. But I am also convinced that in every man, you have—there is, there is a part of a man who is—a human being in his mind—a room that is holy. That is, that is very special. Very high. Very secret room that is—that is a holy part of the human being. (p. 32)

This holy, secret, special, very high room in man, this ineffable holy reality of the human spirit, this great mystery, which is Bergman's furthest experience, is what is carried and symbolized by music in his films.

This "holy part," Bergman says, "has nothing to do with a God of any sort." It is not related to any religion, and yet it strongly expresses an experience of connection to a dimension of spiritual reality. But what is it? Perhaps the key to it lies in the fact that knowing it depends upon an experience. An intellectual statement of a doctrinal belief misses it altogether. It involves something that is lost as soon as it is consciously formulated, In this sense Bergman is verifying the ancient discovery of Lao Tze that "The way that can be consciously trodden is not the way." It is something that expresses its reality by being in the background, by suffusing the interstices of things. You feel its presence, but you cannot touch it. Music in the background of a dream-film is indeed a most appropriate symbol for this.

We observe that Bergman's inner experience and his creative work go hand in hand. In the unity of his life with its cycles and problems, Bergman's dream life and the continuity of his creative work in films have not been separable. Each has fed the other. Many individual artworks in the form of a number of separate films have been created, but there has been a unity of development connecting them. They all have been part of the continuity of experiences that have led to a larger sense of spirit at the depth of Bergman's consciousness. Beyond all the specific works that Bergman has created—actually, by means of them—the artwork of his life has been creating itself. It is an emergent, an extra, the opus that is establishing itself, symbolized by music, gradually filling in the contents of that "very high, very secret room that is the holy part of the human being."

As he continues his work, drawing on his personal past and enabling new perceptions of this vision of truth to emerge, the artwork of Bergman's life, his *opus*, keeps on forming and re-forming itself. Drawing on his past, he is moving into a future that unfolds out of the depth of him. It is clear that the experiences that Bergman has had so far have not come to him arbitrarily as a bolt from the blue. They have come to him in the course of the continuity of his work and by means of his successive artworks. Dream after waking dream have combined with outer reality to make one artwork after another in the form of a motion picture. That has been the content, the formative continuity, of Bergman's inner life. From one experience to another he has gone, letting his past express itself, acting and speaking, letting symbols carry him as vehicles self-propelled in a strange, dark world. From one experience to another he has gone, and from each a certain glimmer of light has been gained. Finally, as an emergent of the whole dialectical process, the secret room within himself has been revealed as the holy place within. But not revealed. Merely recognized, for Bergman has long had intimations of the secret, "this very secret room that is a holy part of the human being." We have reason to believe also that those persons in his audiences who have responded to the process of deepening in Bergman's pictures have also had intimations of the "very secret room," and have been waiting for it to show itself. Following the process within a creative person like Ingmar Bergman, it is apparent that a long continuing life and work of dedication are necessary in order to put the actuality of flesh and blood upon an inner reality so intangible that music is its ultimate symbol.

The continuity of this cumulative experience within Bergman has taken place on the symbolic dimension. For its contents are symbols. In that sense, also, it is a dream. The experiences that are the content of his waking creative life are made of the same stuff as dreams are made of. His creativity is a dream, a waking dream, and also more than a dream. Its content is intensely private and intimately personal. But it carries an encompassing image of life that is transpersonal in its meaning. Without saying a word, it indicates to a person how his life is to be lived. Thus Bergman's experience is more than a waking dream. It is a living myth for him. In the midst of all his works, of all the cycles of inspiration, enthusiasm, anxiety and disappointment it enables him to see the reality and keep perspective even when there is nothing visible on the outer level.

This is the nature of myth, that it is beyond all statements of truth. In a person's life it is deeper than and goes beyond the movement of opposites that comprise the dialectic of hope and anxiety. And there is a paradox in it when a living myth comes together with the continuity of creative work in a person's life. New inspirations seem to come as though of themselves, but they are sustained by the living myth that is at the core of the person. The continuity of artworks that form the opus of the life are emergents of the inner process. They are the result of many dedicated efforts carried out in obedience to the demands of the living myth within the person.

Bergman is thus, from the perspective of holistic depth psychology, an indicative instance of how the dialectic of the psyche leads beyond itself in the life of a creative person to intimations of a spiritual dimension of reality. Inward for the imagery, outward for the artworks, unified in the waking dream that coheres each creative act, the continuity of experience brings forth a living myth. Experiencing and expressing this myth, a person may be able to recognize the secret room in himself that is his—or her—own holy place; and here become one with the meaning of life as it unfolds actively in a process that is at once inward and outward. This can sustain what is valid in artistic work and establish a contact with the spiritual dimension that can reach out by means of artworks to the opus of a life in which personal truths show themselves to have transpersonal meanings.

19

The Anxious Wrestler:
A Zen Story
of Psychotherapy

There is a story told in Zen Buddhism that illustrates the effects of Twilight Imaging. It shows how, when the dialectic in the psyche has gone from hope to anxiety, the movement of energies can be reversed using a technique that is, within its Buddhist context, very similar to what we now call Twilight Imaging. It calls for us to go to a level that is deeper than our individual consciousness, there to evoke symbols; and then, rather than analyze the symbols, to use them as vehicles by which we move to an inner place from which we have a larger perspective of life. With our new inner vision we are able to transform the anxieties that occur in human experience.

The hero of the story is a wrestler, Great Waves by name.* He was a man of tremendous physical strength and he was also of great competence in the art of wrestling. He was able to defeat anyone as long as the bout they were engaged in was private and informal. Then no one could beat him. But if it was a formal match before an audience, the weakest wrestler could defeat him. Great Waves became anxious

---

*For an excellent version of this story see Paul Reps, *Zen Flesh, Zen Bones*, Doubleday Anchor Books, New York, 1961.

when he was before an audience when the match became a formal test of his powers. At such times his great competence left him, and all his years of practice seemed to have been in vain.

The setting of this story is Medieval Japan, but it represents a psychological situation that is quite common in our culture as well. We have all heard of professional persons, attorneys for example, who are brilliant in law school but who fade when they must face a judge and jury in a crowded courtroom, or who lose command of their knowledge when they are called upon to use it in disputes or negotiations. Their capacities are excellent, but they become weak when the time for testing comes. In our psychological era, people would be quick to point out to such an attorney that he is suffering from a psychological disability. He would be given a descriptive diagnosis, depending on the concepts of the school of thought that was diagnosing him, and he would be referred to a psychotherapist for treatment.

Living not in modern America but in the culture of Medieval Japan, the wrestler also realized that he had a problem that required the assistance of another person. In the concept of his cultures, he went to a Zen master and there he received a quality of help that is of great significance for modern psychology.

The master first asked Great Waves to tell him his name. Being told, he advised him to enter the temple and remain there in meditation throughout the night. He instructed Great Waves to work and wait until he would become quiet within, and then to call upon an image by which his name would be represented. He was to hold this image firmly and to permit it to extend itself as it wished. He was to encourage it and draw it forth to the fulness of its own nature. He was to let the great waves come and increase, and he was to enter into the waves and become one with them. When he and the waves were one, his problem would be solved.

The wrestler followed the master's advice. He entered the temple and found a private place where he could be silent and meditate. He sat in silence and tried to quiet his mind, but thoughts of many kinds came to him. Thoughts of his wrestling and thoughts of his friends and his problems and his fears came to him, and he could not be quiet. He remained in silence, however, until eventually in a condition of psychic fatigue, his thoughts subsided and he did become still.

When he became quiet inwardly he was able to think about his name, and with it, the present situation of his life. As he thought of it the image representing it came before his mind's eye. Now he saw waves rising and falling in the sea, great waves reaching tremendous heights, breaking with great strength and dissipating in the sea. He remained in meditation and encouraged the waves to roll on, to rise and fall, to enlarge themselves, to break and disappear, to follow the impulse of their nature with perfect freedom. As they did so, they absorbed an ever larger part of his field of consciousness. The waves rising and falling, became the sea, and as the night progressed a mighty ocean was moving back and forth before him and around him.

As the wrestler remained in concentration upon the image of the ocean and as he permitted it to move according to its own nature, it grew larger and larger. It became the reality of the temple in which he was. The waves moved on and on. They swelled and rose and fell again. They washed away the decorations in the temple. The flower vases disappeared in the flood of the sea. The figures used for religious devotions were washed away by the waves. The holy statues were inundated and washed away. Even the figure of Buddha was engulfed by the waves and disappeared. Nothing remained in the temple. Only the mighty ocean rising and falling, and surging onwards in its cycles was present. This was the sole reality. The temple itself disappeared. There was only the ocean, and the wrestler himself was the ocean. He was no longer the person who called himself by the name of Great Waves. Only the ocean itself was present. The ocean was all, and there were individual waves rising and falling upon that ocean.

In the morning the Zen Master returned to the room in the temple where he had left the wrestler in meditation. He observed him for a moment and then patted him on the shoulder. "Nothing can disturb you now," he told him. "You are the waves. Go forth then and wash all that is before you."

The end of the story is a happy one. It is a story of success. The anxious wrestler, the story concludes, did go forth and was no longer fearful. He became the greatest wrestler in all Japan.

There have been several attempts in recent years to present Zen Buddhism to the West as a new kind of religious philosophy. This story, however, indicates its psychological implications quite specifically. Here the Zen person is coming with a problem and with a purpose to which the modern West has become accustomed in the terms of psychotherapy. It brings into sharp relief the principles which give Zen a dynamic therapeutic effect within its own culture. The Zen master was here facing the problem of an anxiety great enough to bring about failure even though the talents and capacities for success were very large. In our time we see that as a psychological problem to be analyzed and diagnosed. But how did the Zen master approach it? He did not attempt to identify the so-called causes of the anxiety. He did not inquire into the problems of childhood, nor did he make a diagnosis that would link the person and the problems. The story indicates nothing of this. It mentions merely that Great Waves described his difficulty to the master, and there is the implication that they discussed it in sufficient detail to make the problem clear.

The master did not ask him how the problem had come

into being. He did not ask him about resentments toward his mother or his father; nor did he ask him to meditate on his rivalries with his brothers and sisters. In fact, he drew the focus of attention away from the outer conditions of life and also away from the terms in which Great Waves was perceiving his problem. He drew the attention away from the wrestler's consciousness of his difficulty and redirected it toward another level of the psyche.

At this other *place* in the psyche, a *deeper* place in the sense that it was *below* or more basic than the surface of Great Waves' self-consciousness, the pressures of the problem were not felt. A totally different quality of experience now entered the situation. It was actually that a new atmosphere was established within the person, encompassing the situation as a whole and setting a new tone for it. This was accomplished by shifting the attention to a different level, enabling the person to reach a different *place* in the psyche. At this depth in psychic space, the situation of the wrestler's life could be seen in a new light, with a new quality of consciousness. The nature of the problem was thus redefined in the eyes of the wrestler himself.

Once the attention had been shifted to the depth level of the psyche, the redefinition of the problem took place spontaneously without any words being spoken. The reason that it could happen without verbal interpretation is that it was a change of place and of perspective that was being brought about. The change in consciousness that was taking place was not a matter of intellectual concepts but of experience. The change in the tone of awareness was actually happening. It was being brought about by the wrestler even though the Zen master did not specifically speak of it. The wrestler was merely given something specific to do—to conceive the present situation of his life, first in thought, and then to let it take the form of images. As the images would enlarge themselves and become symbols the wrestler was to continue with them, letting the symbols serve as vehicles to take him further. By means of the symbols, he would reach a new perspective, a new quality of awareness with which to see the world and his life within it. This new state of consciousness would come about naturally as though by itself and not by self-conscious direction. Specifically it came about through the activities in which the wrestler was engaged on the level of symbolism in his work of meditation.

The essence of the change taking place was a new perspective experienced by the wrestler as he struggled with the question of his life by means of symbols. This perspective was possible in part because the shift in the focus of attention placed him a distance apart psychologically from the environmental sphere of his trouble. He was experiencing his problem of self-consciousness on the surface level of his psyche where the personality touches the outer world. The shifting inward of his attention drew him out of the vortex of the external storm and enabled him to look at it from a vantage point in the inward space of the psyche. He had been drawn downward and inward to get a perspective of distance from the problems on the outer level of his life.

This was one aspect of it, but the new perspective which he achieved involved more than a movement in psychic space. It began with the fact that as Great Waves became aware of his capabilities as a wrestler, he envisioned great successes for himself in that field. A large hopefulness built within him, but it was not a fundamental hope affirming life as a whole. It was hope that had already become specific in the form of a desire for success in the field of wrestling. And hope that has become specific as a particular desire leads to the fear of failure. That is the dialectic within human life by which hope becomes anxiety. Great Waves took his problem to the Zen master only at the point where this dialectical process in him had become anxiety and was inhibiting his abilities. The dialectic had become an anxiety that blocked the further movement of his life. He could no longer function to fulfill the goal that had become his main desire. The response of the Zen Master was not to seek to break the dialectic by entering it. There was too great a chance that while seeking to change it he would be caught by it and be at the mercy of the movement of opposites. Instead he called the Wrestler's attention to the dimension of experience where symbols connect human beings to the underlying unity of life. Based as it was on the psychological dialectic of hope and anxiety the problem which Great Waves faced was subjective to him. By contrast, the image of the surging waters in the ocean of life possessed an objectivity that transcended persons. The image carried a quality of timelessness; it suggested a transpersonal power encompassing the cycles of life and capable of overcoming them. As his experience of the ongoingness of the ocean became increasingly real to him, Great Waves felt the energy of the universe moving through him; and he identified with it. We might better say that he found himself unconsciously participating in the sea of life and that it progressively absorbed him until it became the main factor in his life. The Zen Master perceived this unity of being and thus he assured Great Waves that his inward wrestling had been carried to the point where he was ready now for outward wrestling once again.

20

The Non-Method of
the Master

There is much to be learned from the psychological insight that lay behind the instructions which the Zen master gave. He might have instructed the wrestler to meditate upon some Buddhist doctrine which he felt to be particularly valid; or he might have suggested to him that he meditate upon some other image that had had a healing effect when he had recommended it to someone else. The master might have drawn upon his past experience and observations to suggest either an image or a concept which he would feel to be especially applicable to the individual. It is important to note that he refrained from doing any of that.

Instead he called the wrestler back to the wrestler's own nature. "What is your name?" he asked him. What is your own, special, individual nature as indicated to you by the situation of your life? Meditate upon that. Eventually that meditation was to reach far beyond subjective psychological elements. It would eventually reach a contact with transpersonal realities basic enough to bring about a healing experience of wholeness. The master knew this, but he did not say so. To speak of it at the outset would have been a case of the right thing at the wrong time.

If, for example, he had suggested to the wrestler at the

beginning that he meditate upon an image of the ongoing unity of the sea of life, that would have spoiled the possibility of eventual success. It would have called upon an elemental depth image before the situation in the psyche had deepened enough to be able to absorb it. Confusion and disorder would have resulted then. The correct way to proceed when Great Waves came to him was simply to recall the wrestler to himself; and this was what the master did. By doing this, he set in motion the process of symbolic unfoldment. The depth of his own knowing enabled him to rely upon the principle behind that process to draw the psyche of the wrestler into harmony with itself.

Two aspects of the master's behavior are of particular interest here. One is that he did not insert himself into the experience which Great Waves was to have. He simply got it started, and then he stayed out of the way. The other is that he took care to begin it in terms that were directly related to Great Waves' personal being, as expressed in his name. He did not permit it to be conceived as an abstraction, even though it was eventually to touch the universals of human life. He rooted it in Great Waves' individual existence, and then trusted the process of symbolic unfoldment to reach out of itself and draw into the wrestler's life all that his nature required.

For the image to unfold, it was essential that the master not intervene. It was, after all, not his image that needed to unfold, but the wrestler's image. If he intervened with the intention of helping things along, he would be intruding. He might provide a semblance of success, and perhaps attain it for the wrestler quicker than would otherwise be the case, and thus the wrestler, putting it in modern terms, would be increasing his "ego attainments as a 'helping' person." But if he inserted himself into the development of awareness that needed to take place within the person called, "Great Waves," he would be depriving that development of its integrity. The growth of awareness which Great Waves needed to achieve in order to be healed of his anxiety would then not be authentically his own. Just as a tree cannot grow from any other roots than its own, so the consciousness of Great Waves could not grow integrally from the psyche of his master. It could grow only out of its own experience, in its own rhythm, and with its own framework of imagery.

The master's delicate task was to guide the wrestler in the proper direction without setting the terms or restricting the style of his growth. To achieve this he had first to awaken within Great Waves an awareness of personal being, and to evoke in him an involvement in its symbolic aspects. This he did by directing him to meditate upon his name, leading Great Waves to establish a sense of his own identity. Once that had been done, the process of symbolic unfoldment could be set in motion. Great Waves could then have experiences that took him beyond his personal being, but they were now in their right timing.

There was now an integrity in the growth of Great Waves' awareness as it extended itself into an experience of transpersonal unity on the symbolic dimension. It was personally authentic; and this meant not merely that it had the virtue of honesty, but that it was functionally sound. The experience of participation in the unity of life was personally authentic because it was organically connected to his psychic roots. It derived from his name, from his personal nature, and it proceeded by a pattern of imagery and a rhythm of unfoldment that was inherently his own. Though the experience might eventually carry him to the utmost reaches of reality, it would still be connected at its roots to his personal nature. It could therefore never be abstract and empty, nor could it drift off into space like an inflated balloon. Though it might touch the heavens in spirit, its foundation would be solidly upon earth, tied to humanity in the form of the individual personality in whom the awareness opened and following definite psychological principles.

The modern person who comes asking the meaning of life can learn much from the master's response. The question "What is your name?" is a reminder to take note of who one is and what the essence of one's life situation is. Likewise, the instructions to meditate upon one's own name is an indication that the place to start the search for meaning is right where one is at the very moment of asking. Start where you are and come as you are. That is what the master was saying. Whatever happens to you will then be in accord with your elemental nature.

The forms of this, being individual, are psychological in content. When a modern person asks, therefore, how he can achieve an experience of meaning that will have personal integrity and validity, the answer must be given in terms of the processes and contents of one's own life. Authentic growth in the capacities of spiritual awareness is an aspect of psychological development where the elemental depths of personality are involved.

A specific procedure that a modern person can follow in this regard is to record whatever imagery experiences come to one, whether fleeting images or extended dramatic scenarios, whether seeming foolishness or with obvious associations, whether sleep dreams or waking imagery. Record it all in your Journal without judgment and without censorship.* If you continue this practice night by night and day by day you will gradually build a significant record of the continuity of your unpremeditated, and unconscious inner life. Eventually it will become bulky and contain many pages of script; but it will also contain many *leads* (Journal Feedback leads) to aspects of your life that are calling to you for your further

---

*In the *Intensive Journal* workbook the specific entries are in the *Dream Log* and the *Twilight Imagery Log*.

attention. You will probably find that you recognize these leads best, not when you are first writing them down but when you are reading your Journal entries back to yourself after a while. The analytic interpretation of these dreams and images will not be important at all; in fact, to interpret them analytically will probably be a detour and a detriment to the movement of the process as a whole. Unavoidably it will tend to inject a rationalistic attitude of mind and draw you up to the intellectual surface of consciousness whereas it is best to maintain one's place at the nonrational depths of the psyche while building one's sensitivity to that aspect of life.

The form in which Great Waves met the question: Who am I? was to meditate upon his name, that is he turned his attention to his specific individual existence. The particular method that he followed in accordance with the instructions of his master was to enter into the depths of psychic space by means of the Zen meditation techniques that were well known and accepted in medieval Japanese cultures. It would seem, too, that the fact of his entry into the temple had a symbolic effect upon the wrestler and helped evoke in him a receptiveness to the quality of reality that reveals itself on the dimension of symbols.

When he had succeeded in refocusing his attention to a level of depth in himself, the name of Great Waves took representational form as an image. This image, which included the waves and the ocean, was obviously suggested by the verbal content of his name. That was only the representational aspect of it, however. The important aspect of the image was the process of symbolic movement which it set in motion. If Great Waves had not been a person whose name carried a specific representational image, he would have drawn an equivalent image representing his life and his identity from the depth of his personal nonconscious perceptions. Several easily available Journal exercises would give him the means of doing this. One would call for him simply to refer to his earlier dreams and images. Another Journal exercise, a brief period of Twilight Imaging after considering his life* would have provided appropriate images.

The essence of the process in which Great Waves was engaged was an active movement of imagery starting with an image that represented to the person his, or her, own life and individuality. It would thus be an image that carried a symbolic correlation to the particular life. Given that starting point, the nature of the active process of imaging at the twilight level would necessarily take the image beyond the limited form with which it began. By means of Twilight Imaging, the symbol would unfold. Starting with the personal, it would move toward becoming more than personal. This process of symbolic unfoldment was expressed in the experience that Great Waves had in the temple. Beginning with the image of waves that was an image personal to him representing his life and his individual nature, the image of waves in its first form was a symbol of his personal life, and then it unfolded to larger-than-personal forms.

The image of the waves was the first phase of a symbolic process in which the fundamental factors of his life were expressed. That it became the image of the sea of life is only because the entry into depth began with the verbal image of his name as Great Waves. We see the principle of unfoldment that lies at the core of symbolic experience operating here. Beginning with the waves, it extended itself spontaneously, image by image, until it became the encompassing, ongoing sea of life. The symbol unfolded from the seed latent in it, proceeding from the particular image by which its individuality was expressed to the ever more generalized and

---

* In the workshops that use the *Intensive Journal* process, this step of "considering one's life" takes the form of listing the Steppingstones of one's life, then reading them back and following the "leads" to the particular aspects of one's life. See *At a Journal Workshop*, p. 98ff.

universal. Eventually it became in imagery form the encompassing unity of life, connecting the individual and the
universe.

This is the principle inherent in the dynamic movement
of symbols. Their style of unfoldment follows tendencies that
appear with such regularity as to suggest that a structural
pattern, or law, is involved. This pattern is the movement
from the particular images that derive from an individual
life to the elemental symbol in which a universal principle is
expressed. When a flow of imagery begins, an image that is
drawn from a personal frame of reference is what gets things
into motion. The initial impetus and need gives the energy
with which the process begins. It is personal, and the symbols begin by being personal. As the twilight movement proceeds, however, the imagery steadily widens itself. The
images that were originally derived from individuality are
absorbed into larger-than-personal, elemental images which
tend to express in symbolic form a person's perception of
ultimates in the situation of human life. These perceptions
may be referred to, alternately, as ontological, metaphysical,
archetypal, symbolic realities. They often become the content
of doctrinal beliefs, which remain fixed for a while but then
may be enlarged in the range of questions that they address
as the process of inner experience on the symbolic level is
continued.*

The elemental symbols absorb the original images with
which the flow had begun. They enlarge then, and the entire
format is progressively restructured from within. It appears
that the importance of the personal form of the imagery lies

---

*The sections of the *Intensive Journal* workbook that are especially devoted to
extending inner experience and exploring the possibilities of enlarging one's doctrinal beliefs are: *Peaks, Depths, and Explorations* and *Inner Wisdom Dialogue.*
The former is among the purple sections for Process Meditation. The latter is
among the blue sections on the Depth Dimension.

in the role it plays in initiating the process as a whole and giving it an individual focus. It begins the process by which a flow of symbolic material comes as from a fountain that draws upon ever greater depths. Once the flow is opened it pours forth more and more, coming from deep sources in the person. The personal symbols are vehicles moving toward a transpersonal awareness by means of Elemental Symbols. That is the process that was set into motion in the experience of Great Waves. He began with a personal image, an image of limited significance when taken by itself. When he entered the temple, however, and when he redirected his energies and his attention to the psychic space within himself, the principle of symbolic unfoldment began to operate. Then the image of the waves enlarged and deepened itself, absorbed all the personal, outer-derivative images that came into its path—images such as his personal anxieties, the decorations in the temple, the holy statues of the Buddha—and finally it became the all-encompassing sea of life.

Beginning with the personal imagery of each individual life, all the roads of inner experience lead back through their symbols to a unitary awareness. All the religions give signs of this connective experience. Whatever the doctrines or disciplines that we follow, it is essential that the work be done with dedication and devotion. We must remain within the terms of our doctrines, whatever they be, for they provide the symbols that can unfold for us from the particular to the universal. At the same time we must remain open to the spontaneity of events so that they can expand our perceptions within the framework of our doctrines. Especially if our path is a personal one—as it is bound to be in modern civilization—it is essential that we not lose perspective while we are in the midst of the journey. We have to remember that a creative principle of life is unfolding by means of the symbols that are working within our experience *behind our minds.* An active process is operating under its own direction and by it the symbols within us are unfolding from the personal to ultimate and universal forms. As the symbols enlarge themselves, they become the vehicles of messages. It is for us then to recognize their message, to absorb them into our consciousness and into the conduct of our life. For this it is essential that we pay attention to the images that come to us even when they seem to be strange and fleeting and too flimsy to follow.

It is essential that we remember that the kaleidoscope of imagery in the psyche is the carrier of the transitory and illusory forms by which a principle of reality unfolds and makes itself available for inner experience. While it is important that we take note of them and record them, we should not make the error of treating these passing images as though they were intended to have a lasting life. We should not make a thing of them; but neither should we pass them by. Symbols are vehicles, and therefore they are leading elsewhere. It is essential that we take note of them as they occur, bearing in mind that it is by means of these images that the great life-sustaining symbols progressively disclose the larger-than-personal meaning of our lives as individuals.

The fleeting images that appear upon the screen of the mind's eye fill the kaleidoscope level of the psyche. They are, at one and the same time, of lasting significance and also of only passing interest. In some ways they may be compared to the short-lived insects of summer by whose passing efforts the flowers grow. The images pass but their movement carries and builds the momentum by which the deep and elemental symbols grow, until they finally burst open like buds. This bursting of the symbol is the moment when the mystery of spirit opens and reveals itself in the life of man, however fleetingly. Sometimes it happens and no one even notices;

sometimes it leads to a new faith, or a work of art. But, whether it is noticed and given fanfare or not, a great power comes into the world when the bud of an elemental symbol opens in an individual life. It is such a power to which the story of the anxious wrestler is pointing and to which it is calling each of us who wrestles anxiously with life.

21

The Judgment of
the Rabbi

In a style that parallels the Zen story of the anxious wrestler and also complements it, a story is told in the Hasidic tradition of Judaism about two families who had a dispute in eighteenth-century Poland. It seems that a member of one of the families was accused of damaging some property of the other family and the issue was creating a great disturbance among all of them. The two fathers argued; the mothers shouted at one another, the many children fought with each other, and the situation was getting out of hand. Neither side would give in, and there seemed to be no solution possible. Finally, the two heads of family agreed that they would take their dispute to the local Hasid, who was a wise and pious rabbi, regarded as the holy man of the area; and they would ask him to render judgment.

Accordingly, the two men requested an audience with the rabbi, and at the appointed time came before him with all their retinue of wives and children. The rabbi asked their problem and they answered him, each proclaiming his own righteousness. The rabbi then asked the men each to tell his own story at whatever length he required. Each of them spoke in detail while the rabbi listened intently, his eyes closed. Finally, when the two men had finished, the rabbi himself began to speak, and all the members of the two families gave him their rapt attention as they listened for his verdict.

He began by telling them how interesting he had found their stories. While he was listening to them, he said, he could not help thinking also of the situation of the Children of Israel when they were in bondage in the land of Egypt. They also had had many arguments there, not only with Pharaoh and their Egyptian taskmasters, but arguments among themselves as well. He was reminded of this particularly, he said, because the time of year was nigh when they would be called upon to remember and celebrate the events in Egypt. He could not help thinking, as they were talking, of the holy days of the Passover season soon to come.

The rabbi then went on to describe to them the thoughts that had come to his mind while each had been stating his case. He had thought of Moses as an infant alone in the rushes of the Nile with his sister Miriam anxiously watching him from the shore. He had thought of the miracle that had made a place for the slave-born baby in the house of Pharaoh's daughter and of the blessing that had followed him when he had left Egypt in exile. He had thought of the burning bush and the word of God calling Moses, the miracles in Egypt, the deliverance, the struggles, the wanderings in the wilderness, the promised land, and the prophecies which they were even now fulfilling in their dispersion among the peoples of the earth.

When the rabbi had finished talking, the two families said, "Amen," which is a way of saying "Yes" with religious feeling. They thanked him for having spoken to them and for having solved their difficulty with such sagacity. All the members of the families then shook hands with one another, blessed each other, wished each other health, long life, and a fortunate year. Then they departed, well content with the wondrous wisdom by which their dispute had been settled.

It was not an illusion. The dispute had indeed been settled. The two families were in conflict no more, and the spirit of argument was gone from their hearts. To this extent the story illustrates a miracle of another kind, the miracle of the transformation of conflict into harmony in the life of human beings. It is a miracle with a principle behind it.

What had happened? The two families were composed of individuals who were engrossed in the everyday tasks of life. As individuals in a small and poor community, their personal needs were primarily to earn their livelihood, care for their children, and to try to secure some status and property for themselves. The pressure of these needs was felt at the outer edges of their personalities, the place where the ego meets the environment and struggles with it to establish its social identity. Here, where egos are insecure, they contend with one another and bring about the unending conflicts in society where one human being is pitted against another.

The dispute which the two families took to the rabbi was experienced upon this outer environmental level of life. The rabbi met it there. He accepted it as a fact and he neither scolded nor blamed them. He did not judge his fellow human beings. He began by permitting the conflict to express itself within its own terms upon the level where its main intensity was being felt. He accomplished this by encouraging each side to state its case as fully as it wished in order that the emotions of conflict might be expressed and thereby might be released.

As the heads of the families presented their individual statements, each maintained his own righteousness against the other and each affirmed his own ego. There was a satisfaction in this, a strengthening as well as a quieting of spirit. When the main blasts of egoistic energy had been allowed to expend themselves, the dangerous intensity of the conflict was neutralized; it could no longer explode. The possibility of a change in the situation was thus established. To describe it

in other terms, its venom having been drawn, it could then
be tamed.

The rabbi could now proceed to shift the focus of attention of the contending parties. He was preparing to conduct
them to a different dimension of awareness, a level on which
their conflict would appear in their own eyes as inconsequen-
tial. Their dispute would not be judged; it would simply disappear from sight. Suddenly it would not be there. They
would not see their conflict any longer because the focus of
their attention would be elsewhere.

In order to induce the quality of attention which was required, the rabbi had to proceed indirectly. He could not tell
them in advance what he intended to do to resolve their
problem. He had to begin by letting them hold the impres-
sion that he was going to give them the kind of answer they
came expecting; and gradually he would readjust their inward vision. Only in this way would a full and fundamental
resolution of their dispute be possible.

When the rabbi spoke, he began by referring to the situation before him. This personal conflict was not unique, he
told them. It had a parallel; indeed, it had many precedents
in Biblical history. Thus the frame of reference was switched
from the small world of self-righteous egos to the large universe of sacred time in which God and man hold their continuing dialogue. This change in the focus of attention
involved a shift from one level of the psyche to another.
Whereas the situation had been experienced upon the outer
environmental level of individual personality where the realities of life are perceived in terms of ego-desires and self-
assertion, the level of experience was now placed at the
transpersonal depth of the psyche.

This involved much more than a different way of thinking about the problem. It meant, indeed, that the experience
of the situation was drawn to a deeper level, and that the
terms in which it was seen would be changed. The facts of

the outer situation would remain the same, but the perception of them would be different. They would not be thought about analytically. They would not be reconsidered, discussed, and judged. The rabbi had no intention of giving them more intellectual insight into their conflict. He wished to change the situation by enabling them to see it from another perspective. To do this, he had to draw them out of it momentarily, at least long enough to readjust their psychic vision so that they could look at it anew from the vantage point of the symbolic dimension. If he could make it possible for them to reenter the situation in symbolic terms, their experience of it would be intuitive rather than analytical; and with this new quality of perception, the problem would resolve iteself.

The set of symbols that was effective in the situation in which the rabbi was working was the Biblical tradition with its view of the special relation between God and the Israelites mediated by Moses and the Prophets. This was a system of symbolism limited to their particular culture and phrased in their provincial accents. It had the effect, however, of recalling the two families to the elemental aspects of their human condition. By means of the historical symbols, their specific problem was given a larger context. They felt themselves, then, not as petty individuals engaged in a dispute of egos, but as persons participating in a movement of history in which God Himself is taking part. In such a perspective, it was unthinkable to waste time with family arguments. Their perception of the situation was now in terms not of the profane world, but of what Eliade has called, "sacred time."

Their perception of "sacred time" depended upon the symbols in which it presented itself to them. These historical symbols, embodying the Biblical relation between God and man, were inextricably bound to their traditions and to the ritual observances practiced throughout their culture. Because these rituals were practiced by virtually all the members of the community, it was not difficult for the rabbi to activate the Biblical symbols strongly enough so that the situations of daily life could be perceived in terms of them. The elemental symbols then became active in the special cultural forms in which the Jewish community knew them. The activity of the symbols consisted in their power to draw environmental situations into a new context, to give them a new symbolic frame of reference, and thus transform them. This meant drawing personal problems off the environmental level of the psyche and into the depths of psychic space where they could be totally recast in terms of the symbolic elementals of human existence.

In drawing the experience down into the depth level of the psyche, the rabbi, like the Zen master, was intuitively practicing what we have seen to be a basic psychological principle, the deepening of the atmosphere in which the events of human life can be perceived. He was, in fact, making it possible for the psyche to follow its natural tendency, from which it had been blocked by the ego desires and contentiousness of the two families. The inherent mode of the psyche in resolving life problems is to move inward and downward to greater levels of depth within itself. There, in the depths of the psychic space within the individual, ever more fundamental patterns of symbolism are activated, and these absorb as they encompass the environmental problems. The problems of life can then be approached anew in a fresh and open perspective of meaning that has its source at the deep foundations of human personality. More than meaning, the individual derives a new power for living from the energy that is made available by awakening the elemental symbols.

The pattern involved in this is inherent in the functioning of the human psyche. To move from frustration in the outer environment to new resources of insight and strength at the depth levels is the model that underlies the process of personal growth and creativity. This is the pattern that the psyche strives to fulfill whenever it is able. Often it is blocked and an impasse develops between the outer frustration and the inability to move inward and unlock the situation. At such times, assistance is needed to check the psychic pain and to begin the movement inward.

Sometimes individuals who have reached such an impasse are able to loosen it by entering a church, either to sit in silence or to participate in the service. The church, like the temple of Great Waves, becomes an outer embodiment of the inner temple of the psyche. The physical entry into the church then becomes a symbol and it initiates a movement of attention into the depths of the person by which the elemental symbols are activated. The process of growth can then begin anew.

Usually the mere entry into a church, or into the quiet of the psyche, is not sufficient by itself. It is necessary also that a movement of imagery be begun and sustained in order that the depths of the psyche be actively awakened. The psyche itself attempts to do this spontaneously because that is its natural way of expression. Of its own inclination it calls forth dreams and a movement of imagery. What is needed then is an open awareness, a cooperative attitude, and a capacity to draw the flow of imagery onward.

The process of symbolic unfoldment is the essence of the creative growth of personality. It begins with the individual in the present situation of life, whatever that may be, no matter the frustrations of the outer circumstances of life. The frustrations themselves exert an inner pressure that sets the process of deepening and of symbolic unfoldment into motion. It activates a movement of energy that stimulates in turn a flow of imagery in dreams, waking visions, poems, paintings, or other art forms that express the depth of the psyche. At first the contents of this imagery tend to be personal and subjective, closely connected to events in the imediate environment. Steadily, however, as the flow of imagery is sustained, it activates ever more elemental symbols, and these place their imprint upon the style and content of the moving images. As the process deepens, the elemental symbols draw the focus of attention ever closer to the core of being, as we saw in the oceanic experience of Great Waves. Increasingly the individual's relation to his environment expresses not egotistic desires but symbolic experience of the elementals of existence. There is a transpersonal quality, then, in the perception of life and the participation in it. The focus of attention is no longer outer and environmental, but inner and existential. The symbolic dimension of depth within the person becomes the source both of strength and a newly effective directing principle. This makes it possible to see the world in a new light and to live one's life in an enlarged context of meaning.

The act of entering a church or a temple can serve on a symbolic level as the vehicle that carries a human being into an atmosphere of depth. In a comparable way, the presence of a person who is culturally identified with sacred space, or the telling of a story that establishes the atmosphere of sacred space, can have the effect of taking persons into the depth level for their perception of life. It can take them into the twilight place within themselves. This was the way that the Rabbi was able to bring peace where there was conflict among his fellow human beings. It expressed a principle that we can follow in order to bring peace where there is conflict within ourselves.

APPENDIX

I

From Psyche-Evoking
to
Whole-Life Study

There was particular value in the fact that two years separated the Eranos papers of 1963 and 1965, the papers that
are brought together in this volume. Concepts that had been
germinating beneath the surface came to crystalization in
the interim so that they could be formulated and presented
in the 1965 Eranos paper. They led to significant changes in
earlier concepts and they eventually provided the principles
that made it possible to develop the *Intensive* Journal process.
Previous to the 1965 Eranos paper I had been working with
the conception of depth psychology as articulated in my
book, *The Symbolic and the Real*, which had been published
in 1963. The viewpoint articulated there opened a number of
very useful perspectives, but its view of journal work was still
restricted in terms of a "psychological workbook." The free-
ing step beyond that did not become possible until the refor-
mulated statement of depth psychology had taken place in
the Eranos paper of 1965.

The essence of the approach that set the basis for the
further development was stated in *The Symbolic and the Real*
as *psyche-evoking*. There it was described as the active alternative to *psycho-analysis*. Probably the most succinct way to
convey the principles that underlie this distinction is by refer-

ring to the metaphor of the boulder and the stream.* Within
Psycho-analysis there has been the conception that the reason a person is neurotic and unable to function productively
is that an earlier experience has been repressed and has become imbedded in the depth of the psyche where it is lodged
as a boulder that dams up the stream. The energies of personality are thus dammed up, unable to move forward. According to the analytic approach to psychotherapy, the
solution is to be found by chipping away at the boulder until
it becomes small enough to permit the waters of the stream
to pass through. The process of chipping away at the boulder, whatever the conceptual approach, is analysis; for analysis, at its etymological roots, means a breaking up. The
attempt to break up the boulder by analysis—which must
eventually become self-conscious—has been a primary goal
of psycho-therapy during the past two generations. It has
also frustrated the fundamental goal of helping people psychologically in a way that can lead to new spontaneous
creative experiences in life.

There are several reasons for the frustrations inherent in
the fact that analysis does not lead to creativity. There is the
fact, firstly, that chipping away at the boulder is a slow, long
and exceedingly difficult task; and secondly, even when the
boulder has been reduced in size or has been altogether
chipped into pebbles, the stream of personality remains
small and flat and weak. From observing what takes place
even in those cases that are successful, we are drawn to the
conclusion that to succeed in the work of psycho-therapy, the
best approach is not to chip away at the boulder—even if we
can eventually eliminate it altogether—but rather to enlarge
the stream. Our goal is to gain access to the sources of the
stream in such a way as to draw more water into the flow of

---

*This is a metaphor that I first used in an article in *The Atlantic Monthly* entitled, *The Psychology of Personal Growth*, July, 1961, p. 103 ff.

it. Then its bed can deepen and broaden and the stream can become a river with sufficient strength to surge past the boulder. That is the goal of psyche-evoking. Only at those times when the water level is low in the psyche will we need to be aware that the boulder is still present. If we can increase the inner sources and raise the level of the water, the person is freed to expand the areas of activity in life and has more resources to draw upon. The momentum of creativity can then be built in the life, for the boulder will no longer be an impediment.

This metaphor holds the key to our practical approaches, not only to the particularities of Twilight Imaging but to the view of life-in-motion that underlies the *Intensive Journal* process. Its principle is that the creative development of personality is to be achieved not by analyzing individuals but by evoking the depths of them, by stimulating the inner movement of the psyche, thus contacting energy at its source and nurturing the development of the individual through the painful valleys of experience until the seed-potentials can unfold.

The distinction between psyche-evoking and psychoanalysis was primarily derived from experiences I had had in the practice of psychotherapy. There I had encountered what is a very common problem in the practice of psychotherapy, namely, the difficulty in getting a movement started when a person is in a stopped position, at an impasse in life with nothing in motion. At that point the person will often have developed an attitude that accepts the fact of life being at a standstill, and this attitude becomes a major hindrance. The primary task then is to have a means of generating energy from a place in the person's psyche that is beyond any of the attitudes or habits that have led to the stoppage. And yet it must be within the context of the individual life and its interests so that, once the movement has been begun, it will have a framework within which it can continue and build its own momentum.

In a situation that needs to develop movement, the approach of analysis tends not to be helpful because the analytic mode carries with it an attitude of acceptive understanding that is inherently passive rather than active in relation to the contents of a life. It builds an attitude of knowing *about* something rather than actively being involved in it and extending it. The opposite approach is to stimulate the depth of a person so that greater resources will be available to supply energy and also to supply the materials for life-decisions. It is essential not only that this new material come from a depth within the person but that it express the context of the life, its interests and contents, giving data with which one may reconsider the direction of the life-movement that had earlier come to a halt.

In order to activate the movement of life-data at the depth of the person I had developed the technique of Twilight Imaging, extending in this regard the work of C. G. Jung, Otto Rank and Henri Bergson. I used the Twilight Imaging technique to evoke the depths of the Organic Psyche in persons, being careful to avoid intruding myself and even inadverdently directing the flow of the imaging. Working within the context of the individual life, it was important not to intrude into the other person's twilight experience. Following this guideline, psyche-evoking led to a number of valuable experiences, some of which were described in the book, *The Symbolic and the Real,* and other places. At that time experimentation with psychedelic drugs was much in vogue, and many persons were using drugs of various kinds, especially LSD, to stimulate deep and "spiritual" experiences. Because of my published point of view in which I recommended an approach of *evoking* the psyche rather than analyzing it, many of the drug experimentors assumed that I would be in favor of the psychedelics. At first people seemed to have only "good" trips with LSD, but as the novelty wore off and as the side-effects began to be felt, there were an increasing number of "bad" trips.

My point of view was that, as we now recognize that the answer to many psychological problems lies in getting access to more material from the depths of the person not to analyze but to feed into the process of growth, it is possible to do this without ingesting physical substances that may be alien to our bodies and can have a negative effect. I was thinking of the "bad" trips that were increasingly being reported, although the negative physical effects of LSD had not yet been substantiated; and I was thinking of the use of Twilight Imagery as a means of evoking the depths of the psyche without resorting to physical stimulants.

Whether this perspective influenced any of the LSD enthusiasts I do not know, but it had an important effect on my own thought. It led me to consider that to the degree that it was true that Twilight Imaging can evoke deep inner experiences equal to those stimulated by psychedelic drugs, it can also have other effects. Observing the varieties of experiences that persons had, I inferred that one of the results of depth imagery, whether set into motion by a drug or not is that it could stimulate aspects of the life out of relation to the context of the life as a whole. This seemed to me to be the main psychological problem that persons experienced in using LSD, apart from the physical side-effects; the drug experience in many cases stimulated a movement of depth material that moved out of relationship to the situation of the life. In this regard I had the experience when I was teaching at Drew University that several students who had had "wonderful" LSD trips during the summer audited my seminars in the fall. Their trips had been "wonderful" but they were now not able to function in their lives. My conclusion was that their experiences may indeed have been wonderful with respect to the exciting imagery that had been stimulated, but it had not

taken place in the context nor in the timing of their lives. As
a result they were subject to feelings of confusion and dis-
orientation that prevented them from functioning even at a
minimum level in the actualities of their lives. At least tem-
porarily that condition could be diagnosed in terms of
psychosis.

These observations seemed to me to be the key to any
negative possibilities that might be involved in any technique
that would stimulate the movement of imagery at a depth
level. Whether or not physical drugs were used, it was essential that the person be working in the context of his or her
life. The context of the movement of the life both at inner
and outer levels not only provided a protection in the case of
using psychedelic drugs, it also provided a framework into
which new depth experiences could be fed. It provided a
means of getting the benefits of Twilight Imaging whether
psychedelic drugs were used or whether the method relied
altogether on psychological rather than physical means,
using Twilight Imaging in the context of the Organic Psyche.

Considering the concepts and experiences we already
had, it was not difficult to provide the protection and the
framework that was needed, that would make the subjectivities of individual life tangibly available for personal work.
This was the *Intensive Journal* workbook. But more impor-
tantly, before the *Intensive Journal* workbook could provide
an operable method, it was essential to have a perspective in
which each individual's life could be seen as a whole in its
movement and timing. This would provide the framework
and be the basis for stimulating the movement of imagery in
the depth of a person. Twilight Imaging had to be done in
the context of a person's life as a whole. This was a fundamental conclusion with large implications. It was reached
during the two-year interim between the Eranos paper of
1963 and that of 1965. As much as anything, it was this conception of the whole life history in relation to the twilight

depths that made it possible to develop the *Intensive Journal* process and eventually the nonanalytic Journal Feedback method.

As things turned out, the steps that were taken to establish a perspective for the movement of each individual life led to a conception of the whole life of a person seen as unfolding out of a seed-depth by means of dialectical factors. Much of this is expressed in the Eranos paper of 1965. Once a perspective had been developed for working in one's life as a whole, the next step was to have a structured Journal (the *Intensive Journal* workbook, as it turned out) that would make it possible to work tangibly with the several contents within a life, each with their varied timings. Eventually when the *Intensive Journal* workbook had been developed as an instrument by which an individual could work with his or her life as a whole, the Journal exercises for using it led to the experience of Life Positioning, placing oneself within the moving context of one's life between one's past and one's potentials. It led also to Journal Feedback as the necessary nonanalytical way of absorbing twilight imaging into the movement of the life as a whole.

The framework of thought that was developed in the Eranos paper of 1965 thus opened the way for the *Intensive Journal* process. The 1963 paper had taken as its starting point the depth psychology of psyche-evoking which sought to draw from the depths of the psyche the resources and guidance for meeting the problems of the individual life. But events in society made it clear that Twilight Imaging by itself can be misleading. The very power that is contained in the depth of the human psyche can lead to symbolic overbalancing and can cause the individual to topple over in the world. This was the observation that led in the 1965 Eranos to developing a framework for understanding the unfoldment of a whole life, first on a conceptual level and a little later on a practical level by means of the *Intensive Journal* process. In the more recent developments Twilight Imagery has continued to play a major role, as it did in the practice of psyche-evoking. It gives access to the inner resources that are deep within the person. Now, however, the imagery experiences are set within the context of the movement and contents of the life as a whole. Whatever one finds in the depth of one's life can be placed in a larger context of thought and helped to give its message by means of the *Intensive Journal* method.

One aspect of the two Eranos papers that are brought together here is that the continuity between them formed the concepts that underlie the *Intensive Journal* method. Beyond that, however, is the relation between the principles of Dialectics and those of Depth Psychology. It is by the dialectical movement of opposites that the depth processes of hope inherently lead to anxiety, and then go beyond anxiety to creativity again. The principles of Dialectics are the means by which the depths of the psyche are creative. It is important for us to understand this and to experience its workings in the specifics of life. Dialectics becomes depth in action as the interplay of opposites within persons generates an energy that becomes a creative factor in the world. Understanding the principles that are involved in this is essential if we are to use the *Intensive Journal* instrument fruitfully in our lives.

II

Qualitative Time
in
Reconstructing a Life

When the perspective of depth psychology was extended to cover a full life span as a means of establishing the context for the movement of a person's whole life, the periods in a life were first marked off chronologically. The first way of approaching the subject was in terms of the physical passage of years. That was good as a starter. It provided a means of drawing together the basic life data while articulating some essential concepts. But it soon needed to be changed.

The value of a chronological approach for starting to build a perspective of the transitions within a life is apparent in the pages of the Eranos paper of 1965. It provides a framework for gathering the objective data of life. But the aspects of a life that make each life unique are not objective. Experience with the *Intensive Journal* process has called our attention to an aspect of human life other than the chronological that has turned out to be both more relevant and helpful for the task of establishing a perspective for the movement within an individual human life. This is each person's subjective relation to the movement of time in the life. In the development of the concepts that underlie the structure of the *Intensive Journal* workbook and the Journal exercises this is called "qualitative time." Its philosophic rootage lies in the work of Henri Bergson. At the practical level of using the *Intensive Journal* method for positioning oneself in the movement of one's life, the section of the *Intensive Journal* workbook that embodies the conception of "qualitative time," is *Steppingstones.* The exercises in this section make it possible for a person to reconstruct his or her life spontaneously as well as briefly, going from the time of birth to the present time in the life, without having to worry about whether all the facts have been included and whether the listing is "correct."

Since the Steppingstones are listed from a subjective point of view, there is no question about objective correctness. It is not a need, and therefore is not an issue. Our experience over the years has demonstrated that the factor of the greatest importance in the reconstruction of a life is the "finewinding," the drawing together in a compact form of the events in the individual life. This is achieved easily by listing the Steppingstones of the life from time to time together with those of the other Journal exercises that extend and fill in the details of the Steppingstones. It should be noted that the leads that are drawn from one's Journal Feedback work may be especially valuable in this regard.

The primary purpose in listing the Steppingstones by the particular procedures that have crystallized in the course of using the *Intensive Journal* process is to mark off the "thread of continuity" within the movement of a life. Doing this enables a person to draw out of the varied events that comprise a lifetime those particular events and interests that relate to the needs of the situation at hand. In this regard the Steppingstones exercises often function in a way that is comparable to certain kinds of dreams. By means of them the person is able to establish a present position with respect to the personal past and the possibilities of the future. The Steppingstones exercises place a person at the mid-point of time, between the past and the future; and thus they can be very helpful in moving through the transitions that are inherent in the changes of life.

It is implicit both in the conception of "qualitative time" and in the Journal exercises for working in the Steppingstones section that the experience of being at a mid-point in time is always subjective. All through one's life there are mid-points in time; and at each point one can establish a current position. But each mid-point is different. Even though it is the same person's life, each mid-point places the person at a different position in life. The situation is different and the perception is different; subjectively as well as chronologically, the time is different. In this regard Heraclitus pointed out long ago that while it is always the same river, we never step in the same water twice. And William James, in modern American times, pointed out that the moment in time that we have just called the "present," has now gone past us and is already the past. What used to be our future is now our present, and will be our past in another moment. It was this perception that led James to speak of the "specious present." The conception of "qualitative time" with its corresponding Journal exercises that are carried out in the Steppingstones section and in other sections of the Life/Time Dimension (the red sections) of the *Intensive Journal* workbook are intended to provide a tangible means of working with and exploring the possibilities of our subjective perceptions of life. It is essential that we work with our subjectivities, and that we do so as objectively as we can while proceeding in a non-self-conscious way.

One purpose of the *Intensive Journal* method is to incorporate within a single methodology the opposites of subjective and objective that are inherent in the conduct of a human life. Developing the study of individual lives involves a special use of the dialectical approach and calls for a very particular use and practice of our depth understanding.

One reason for the importance of subjectivity when work-

ing in the field of human life histories and personal development is Herman Hesse's observation that each human
being's life is unique, i.e., that the combination of contents in
each life is different from the combination in every other
person's life. But there are a number of additional reasons of
both a theoretical and practical nature. Persons who wish to
follow the development of thought and the reasons for moving in the *Intensive Journal* process away from the chronological reconstruction of a life to the conception of "qualitative
time" and the corresponding Journal exercises now used in
the Life/Time dimension of *Intensive Journal* work may follow the references that are given below to the various texts
used for the *Intensive Journal* process.*

I should here add the observation that with the perspective of time and retrospect in the conduct of *Intensive Journal*
programs it has become increasingly clear that the single
most important conceptual factor in making the *Intensive
Journal* process helpful to modern persons is the view of
"qualitative time" together with the Journal exercises that derive from it. This point was brought home strongly to me
when I was developing the Life-Study approach that applies
the *Intensive Journal* process to the study of the lives of persons from history. In that work we serve as Journal Trustees
for persons from any part of history; but they are always
persons who are no longer living. When Life-Study was being
developed the question arose briefly of whether it would be
best to use exercises based on objective chronological time or
the Journal exercises based on subjective qualitative time.
Considering our experience in the use of *Intensive Journal*
techniques, there was little room for questioning. It was
clear that "chronological time" was a useful concept at a very
early point in the study of lives, but it has outlived its useful-

---

*Cf. *At a Journal Workshop*, pp. 98–157; *The Practice of Process Meditation*, pp.
39–86; 128–170; *Life-Study*, pp. 70–103.

ness. Experience has confirmed the fact that procedures for the study of lives in terms of qualitative time carry a dynamic that moves toward holistic integrations.

Subjective approaches yield results that are very difficult to quantify but after a while they do give objective results. Eventually, as we proceed with them, we find ourselves in a position to make observations about them that have a quality of objectivity, and these can be quantified if need be. What is most important is that by these techniques we do not falsify the subjectivity that is inherent in individual human existence. Rather we honor and work with the subjectivity of human life, and by this means we are able to enter an area of life experience that would otherwise be limited to those participating in the creative arts. But that may indicate one of the reasons why the *Intensive Journal* approach has been so widely used by persons engaged in the creative arts; and why the fundamental conception in the *Intensive Journal* method is to approach a modern life as a potential artwork.

III

Utopia
and
Utopian Persons

In the Eranos paper of 1963 dealing with *The Dynamics of Hope and Utopian Persons,* considerable mention was made of the term, "Utopia." Speaking of it at the conference that year provided an opportunity to consider the social aspects of depth psychological work, including the important connections between individuality and history. In my discussion of it, I was led to an awareness of a particular kind of personality, the Utopian Person, whose goals of life extend beyond individuality and often beyond self-seeking, even though the style of thought is not only secular but is often antagonistic to any aspect of language or symbols that have the overtones of spirituality. Increasingly we have come to realize that the non-judgmental approach of the *Intensive Journal* process can provide a useful tool for these self-less and secular Utopian Persons.

There are substantial social benefits to be gained, but language continues to be a hindrance. Although it had a very respectable usage in past centuries, nowadays when the term, "utopia" is used, it tends to draw a disdainful response. This is primarily because it has come to be associated in the modern mind with an unrealistic and impractical view of society.

That inference is not correct, however. In its etymology, the word, utopia, derives from roots that give it the meaning of no-place. The use of the word therefore always implies that the person using it knows that it refers to a place or to a human condition that does not exist in actuality. The contents of society that are described or are hoped for in speaking of utopia are not thought of as actually being in existence or as necessarily being possible. They are goals for the future. They are the standards for the future. They carry the criteria by which decisions can be made that will establish the conditions for the future. Although by definition Utopia does not exist in actuality since it is inherently a no-place, it possesses a great practical importance. It states the terms, and especially the ideals, by which the future can be formed. To that degree the image of utopia can have a large effect upon the present moment in society because it contains the hopes and the criteria by which the movement from the Now Moment can be drawn toward the future.

In every period of history there are some individuals who are particularly attracted by an image of utopia that they experience in the depth of themselves. Very often this feeling sets them at odds with the human beings who are close to them. This happened in the life of Leo Tolstoy. It is not difficult to make a diagnosis of such persons and to dismiss them because of their utopian feelings. If we do not dismiss out of hand, however, the visionaries who are the Utopian Persons in each period of history, and if we can help them set their imagery in the context of actualities that are seeking to unfold in society, we will find that we have added a resource to the human species. We will eventually have reason to be glad that Utopian Persons are part of the human species. But we will have to be patient with the process that is unfolding by means of their lives, as we learn that we often have to be patient with ourselves. That is one of the significant messages that emerges from our exploration of hope and the way that it moves into a phase of anxiety in the course of the dialectics of life.

We have seen how the principle of opposites has been at work in the movement from depth psychology to the formation of the *Intensive Journal* process. On the one hand the principles of dialectics enabled us to establish the structure of thought by which the *Intensive Journal* process could be established. On the other hand these principles are the source of problems that persist in human existence; and these are problems that the *Intensive Journal* method must be able to resolve. We see the problems arise in the dialectic of hope and anxiety. They are inherent in the movement of opposites as the tensions of time cause hope to move into the valley of anxiety. In the Eranos paper on *The Dynamics of Hope* I called upon the philosophic perspectives of Meister Eckhart and Paul Tillich to provide an answer to anxiety. But the subsequent development of the *Intensive Journal* process has given us tools that are more specific than philosophy tends to be. The structure of the *Intensive Journal* workbook provides particular Journal exercises to enable Utopian Persons to work out the details and problems of their visions for humankind. There are specific ways for Utopian Persons to use their Journals as instruments for their lives in such *Intensive Journal* sections as: *Dialogue with Society; Dialogue with Works; Peaks, Depths and Explorations; Inner Wisdom Dialogue.* There is a great deal that is possible for Utopian Persons because the *Intensive Journal* method is non-judgmental but is open enough to encompass the largest goals of humankind.

IV

Evocative
Science and Art

The distinction between declarative and evocative sciences
has many implications for the process of education in modern society. Where education has the goal of preparing
persons to work at helping other human beings, whether
professionally or not but definitely with something more to
offer than good intentions, the evocative sciences tend to become evocative arts. It is this perception that led me to see
the importance of having an encompassing conception of
Humanic Arts to supply the framework for the various aspects of education. In that context the special quality of the
evoking arts is that they seek to stimulate the twilight level in
human beings on the basis of proven knowledge that has
been gathered in the sciences.

Eventually this becomes the essence of the distinction between the arts and sciences; and it is the heart of the problem
in teaching them. The arts make use of knowledge that has
been gathered by the declarative sciences—as the Medical
Arts make use of biology and chemistry, and as the Technological Arts adapt physics and chemistry. Where applications of declarative science involve the development of
human beings, we have to speak to the Humanic Arts. Depth
psychology plays a significant role in that, and that is one

reason for the difficulties that arise in teaching it on a general level. Teaching an evocative science is not the same as teaching a declarative science. The subject cannot be learned simply by having the concepts described. They must be experienced inwardly in terms of one's own life, thereby linking objective knowledge and subjective experience.

The problem becomes more complicated as well as more significant when our understanding of the nature of depth psychology is expanded. When depth psychology is thought of in terms of psychiatry, as it has been since its inception in the nineteenth century, the problem of education is not very difficult. In that context education that has depth psychology as its main subject is primarily for professional purposes. It is to explain and provide the means of dealing with particular emotional illnesses. These illnesses concern the emotions, and to that degree they share in the needs of personal experience. But when depth psychology is seen in its larger and essential scope as dealing with the whole lives of persons, more than knowledge for professional use is involved in the subject matter. It is then the conduct of life, the cycles of whole life experience, that are at issue. In that context the concern of depth psychology is with persons not as "case histories" but as "life histories." The subject is human beings and the problems that arise from the fact that each person has a unique individual destiny to be lived.

In the years since the distinction between declarative and evocative sciences was made, important steps have been taken toward teaching depth psychology in terms of the personal life experience of human beings. The basic step has been the conception of the Humanic Arts which undertakes to establish a framework for applying holistic depth psychology in the areas of study and practice where human beings are seeking to be of help to other human beings especially to assist in the creativity and conduct of their lives. The Humanic Arts concept opens several possibilities in university situations.

Essential for the Humanic Arts is the conception and method of Life-Study which uses the *Intensive Journal* process as its model and basic method for entering the lives of persons who have already lived and died. The Life-Study approach calls for individuals to be Journal Trustees for the person whose life they choose, and then to set up an *Intensive Journal* workbook in the first person on behalf of that person in order to reconstruct their life using the *Intensive Journal* process in a specially adapted form as the guide. We have found that the experience of being a Journal Trustee enables a person to participate in the life of another person and to move through the cycles of their life experience, thereby acquiring some additional sensitivities and awarenesses both of the pitfalls and the possibilities of wisdom in the conduct of one's own life. Life-Study, as a means of participating in whole lives from birth to death, is beginning to give us its benefits. One of these is in building an enlarged vision of depth psychology as an evocative science within the general field of the Humanic Arts, thus providing not only a knowledge of the cycles of human behavior but a means of gathering wisdom for the conduct of life.*

---

*See Ira Progoff, *Life-Study*, Experiencing Creative Lives by the *Intensive Journal* method, Dialogue House Library, New York, 1983.

Index

ABOUT THE AUTHOR

Since the early nineteen-fifties Dr. Progoff has been exploring psychological methods for creativity and spiritual experience in their social applications. He is the creator of the widely accepted *Intensive Journal* method of personal development and its related approach of Process Meditation.

The sources of the *Intensive Journal* method are contained in a trilogy of Ira Progoff's earlier books. *The Depth and Rebirth of Psychology* (1956) crystallizes the cumulative results of the work of Freud, Adler, Jung and Rank to form the foundation for a new psychology. *Depth Psychology and Modern Man* (1959) presents a holistic view of evolution as the foundation for a non-analytic method in Depth Psychology. *The Symbolic and the Real* (1963) describes the role of an active psychology for modern society as it demonstrates the personal use of Twilight Imagery.

Drawing on the principles described in these books, the *Intensive Journal* method emerged in 1966 as a non-analytic, integrative system for drawing forth and interrelating the contents of an individual life. After being tested in practice, the underlying concepts and techniques were set forth in *At a Journal Workshop* (1975). This book received the Medical Self-Care Book Award for psychology in 1978 as "The best book on psychological self-care we've seen." In 1980 *The Practice of Process Meditation* described the use of the *Intensive Journal* process as a progressive, non-doctrinal means of enlarging the experience of meaning. These two volumes contain the philosophy and techniques of the *Intensive Journal* method.

In 1983 *Life-Study* was published as a further step in the *Intensive Journal* educational program. It describes the application of the *Intensive Journal* process in experiencing the lives of significant persons from past generations. It is an approach that is increasingly utilized in programs of education for values in the conduct of life.

As the public use of the method increased, the National *Intensive Journal* Program was formed in 1977. It now supplies materials and leaders for the conduct of *Intensive Journal* workshops in the United States and other countries in cooperation with local sponsoring organizations.

Dr. Progoff is currently Director of the *Intensive Journal* program at its Dialogue House headquarters in New York City.